WOMEN
AND MEN

Traditions and Trends

edited by SUZANNE FREMON

THE REFERENCE SHELF
Volume 49   Number 5

THE H. W. WILSON COMPANY
New York   1977

THE REFERENCE SHELF

The books in this series contain rep of articles, excerpts from
books, and addresses on current issues a ocial trends in the United
States and other countries. There are s separately bound numbers
in each volume, all of which are generally published in the same cal-
endar year. One number is a collection of recent speeches; each of the
others is devoted to a single subject and gives background information
and discussion from various points of view, concluding with a comprehensive bibliography. Books in the series may be purchased individually or on subscription.

Library of Congress Cataloging in Publication Data
Main entry under title:

Women and men.

(The Reference shelf; v. 49, no. 5)
Bibliography: p.
1. Sex role. I. Fremon, Suzanne. II. Series.
HQ1075.W66   301.41   77–15960
ISBN 0–8242–0607–X

PREFACE

The subject of women and men, especially in their dealings with one another, has been fascinating and worrisome throughout history. It has also been a major source of humor, sometimes good-natured, often cruel or degrading. In general, the basic assumption has been that women and men are natural adversaries who must accommodate to each other out of mutual need but that the very great differences make the accommodation always difficult.

Anatomical differences are among the major distinctions between the sexes, obvious from birth. But there are many other differences—emotional, psychological, social—which in the view of some are not congenital but are the result of cultural conditioning from birth. Those who hold this view often cite the fact that in various human societies, through the ages and around the world, there is a wide range of activities and personality types considered "typically" or "instinctively" masculine or feminine. Although these activities and personalities differ widely from one society to another, indicating that such behavior may be learned rather than inborn, in most societies these differences—called sex-roles—are clearly defined, enforced, and individually internalized.

Sex-role conditioning in present-day American life is rooted in the Judeo-Christian tradition of patriarchy and, much more recently, in the social mores engendered by the European Industrial Revolution of the eighteenth century. As in any society, this conditioning begins early and is reinforced throughout life.

The first section, introductory in nature, discusses the changing situation of women in recent decades. The second, third, and fourth sections take up the problems faced by both women and men in the stages of their lives, focusing

3

on early conditioning to sex roles and later reinforcement. Section II deals with childhood and early and secondary education, the period when behavioral patterns and attitudes are unconsciously formed. Section III addresses itself to young adulthood, with its special difficulties and opportunities that must be reevaluated in terms of the new awareness of traditional limitations and the emergence of new lifestyles. The situation of older adults, who came of age before this heightened awareness of assumptions rooted in the past, is a concern of Section IV, which focuses on families and careers.

The final section looks not only at the present, with its fresh perceptions of traditional modes, but to a future promising less destructive ways of coping with the problems that vex human beings—ways that will minimize hostility and replace the adversary philosophy with a goal of mutual respect and esteem.

The editor wishes to thank the authors and publishers of the selections that follow for permission to reprint them in this compilation.

SUZANNE FREMON

September 1977

NOTE TO THE READER

For an earlier view of the image and the reality of women's roles in life, the reader is referred to Diana Reische's *Women and Society* (Reference Shelf, Volume 43, Number 6) published in 1972.

CONTENTS

I. BIOLOGY OR CULTURE?

EDITOR'S INTRODUCTION

The Freudian doctrine that biology is destiny gives the sanction of science to a popular belief that was until very recently all but universal. Freud and his followers, especially Hélène Deutsch, held that a woman who rejected her traditional, biologically determined role was automatically at fault. Other schools of thought, however, stress the differences in tradition in other cultures, other eras. What, they ask, is the relative importance of culture—of time and place —in the development of traditional roles perceived as biological?

The problems created by sex-role determinism constitute the theme of this section, which concentrates on the situation of women. (Until now there has been little study of the counterpart situation of men in their role as half of the human race. A critical examination of the *role* of men from this perspective is only just beginning. The *history* of men, on the other hand—as feminists are quick to note— fills the libraries of the world.)

The first article, written in 1941 by the prominent psychiatrist Clara Thompson, records observations of the problems of women in adjusting to what is commonly considered "normal." It is based in part upon the author's experience with patients whose "maladjustments" were thought severe enough to require treatment.

An extract follows from a *Horizon* article by Kenneth Lamott reporting on scientific studies of biological differences involving brain structure, hormones, and chromosomes—differences that manifest themselves in such traits as intellectual ability and aggressive behavior. A defense of traditional social roles as reflections of innate biological

9

differences is then presented by Phyllis Schlafly, a leading opponent of the feminist movement.

The next excerpt, by Betty Friedan, from *It Changed My Life*, is a brief recapitulation of her landmark work *The Feminine Mystique*. That book, published in 1963, is usually credited with sparking the second, or current, wave of the women's movement in America, the first having been the drive for suffrage begun in the nineteenth century. Friedan shows how the glorification of women's traditional role came about in the late 1940s after World War II—a swing of the pendulum away from the tendency of the previous two decades for women to work outside the home.

The last selection, a 1970 address by the famed anthropologist Margaret Mead, describes in sociological terms the widespread, now openly acknowledged malaise of women. In a world that can no longer support a rising population, large numbers of women—and men—can be released from the obligations of parenthood. But society must at the same time continue to provide the best possible care for children and make economic use of the time of women. Child rearing—parental or professional—must be regarded as dignified, treated with respect, and adequately compensated. Mead thus anticipates yet another swing of the cultural pendulum, for the feminists of the late 1970s give full recognition to homemaking as a vocation for women, stressing that women at home are indeed working, that they must be honored for their work, and most importantly that their work earns and must receive due monetary credit.

WOMEN IN THE AMERICAN CULTURE [1]

A comprehensive presentation of the situation of women in this culture is far beyond the scope of this paper. It is a

[1] From paper entitled "The Rôle of Women in This Culture," read before New York Psychoanalytic Society, January 28, 1941, by Dr. Clara Thompson, psychiatrist, lecturer, teacher, writer. *Psychiatry*. 4:1-8. '41. Copyright © 1941 by the William Alanson White Psychiatric Foundation, Inc. Reprinted by special permission of The William Alanson White Psychiatric Foundation, Inc.

task for careful research. The aim here is merely to present observations and speculations on the cultural problems seen through the eyes of psychoanalytic patients. This offers a limited but a very significant view of the situation.

These observations are limited in the first place because for economic reasons psychoanalysis is not yet available to any extent to the lower classes. Secondly, for emotional reasons, groups with strong reactionary cultural attitudes are seldom interested in psychoanalysis. Finally, individuals leading fairly contented lives lack the impulse to be analyzed. This means that we are dealing in this paper chiefly with the ideas and points of view of the discontented, and they happen to be for the most part from the upper classes. Although this is a special group within the culture, it is an important group because, on the whole, it is a thinking group, non-conformist, and seeking to bring about changes in the cultural situation. The study of the types of cultural problems presented by women in analysis thus gives important information about the problems of women in the culture.

There will be no attempt in this paper to make an extensive study of early conditioning and traumatic factors in the lives of women but rather to show how women have found means of expressing their strivings, neurotic and otherwise, in the present culture of the United States.

When Freud first wrote his *Studies in Hysteria* in the 1890s, he described a type of woman with ambitions and prospects very different from those found in the average psychoanalytic patient of today. That a radical change has occurred is partly due to Freud's own efforts in clarifying the whole question of the sexual life, but largely due to changes in the economic and social status of women. These changes were already occurring before the time of Freud.

In this country today women occupy a unique position. They are probably freer to live their own lives than in any patriarchal country in the world. This does not mean that they have ceased to be an underprivileged group. They are

discriminated against in many situations without regard for
their needs or ability. One would expect, therefore, to find
the reality situation bringing out inferiority feelings not
only because of a reaction to the immediate situation but
because of family teachings in childhood based on the same
cultural attitude. One would expect to find, also very frequently, resentment towards men because of their privi-
leged position as if the men themselves were to blame for
this. These are some of the more important factors that contribute to a woman's feeling of inferiority.

As we know, the culture of Europe and America has
been based for centuries on a patriarchal system. In this
system, exclusive ownership of the female by a given male
is important. One of the results has been the relegating of
women to the status of property without a voice in their
own fate. To be sure, there have always been women who,
by their cleverness or special circumstances, have been able
to circumvent this position, but in general, the girl-child has
been trained from childhood to fit herself for her inferior
rôle; and, as long as compensations were adequate, women
have been relatively content. For example, if in return for
being a man's property a woman receives economic security,
a full emotional life centering around husband and children, and an opportunity to express her capacities in the
management of her home, she has little cause for discontent.
The question of her inferiority scarcely troubles her when
her life is happily fulfilled, even though she lives in relative
slavery. If, therefore, the problem of women today simply
referred to their position in a patriarchal culture, the task
would be much simpler. However, without considering the
fact that the individual husband may be unsatisfactory and
so produce discontent, other factors are also at work to
create dissatisfaction. As Erich Fromm has said, "When a
positive gain of a culture begins to fail, then restlessness
comes until a new satisfaction is found." Our problem with
women today is not simply that they are caught in a patri-

archal culture, but that they are living in a culture in which the positive gains for them are failing.

Industry Now Out of the Home

Industry has been taken out of the home. The making of clothes has been entirely removed, and now it is necessary to know only the most rudimentary types of cooking. Factory-made clothes and canned goods have supplanted the industry in the home. Large families are no longer desired or economically possible. Also, other more emotionally tinged factors contribute to the housewife's dissatisfaction. The home is no longer the center of the husband's life. Once he ran a farm or a small business close to his home. In this his wife shared his problems, probably more than he realized. Today, a man's business is often far from his home and his wife's possible contribution to it may be nothing. If one adds to this the fact that the sexual life is often still dominated by puritanical ideas, the position of the present-day wife who tries to live in the traditional manner cannot but be one with a constant narrowing of interests and possibilities for development. Increasingly, the woman finds herself without an occupation and with an unsatisfactory emotional life.

On the other hand, the culture is beginning to offer her something positive in an opportunity to join in a life outside the home where she may compete with other women and even with men in business. In the sexual sphere too, with the spread of birth control knowledge and a more open attitude in general about sex, there is an increasing tendency in and out of marriage to have a sexual life approximating in its freedom that enjoyed by the male. However, these things do not yet run smoothly. In other words, we are not yet dealing with a stable situation, but one in transition; therefore, one in which the individual is confused and filled with conflict, one in which old attitudes and training struggle with new ideas.

Woman's restlessness began to make itself felt about the middle of the last century. Prior to that and even for some time afterwards, the position of woman was fairly clear-cut and stable. Her training was directed towards marriage and motherhood. If she made a good marriage, she was a success. If she made a bad marriage, she must try to adjust to it because it was almost impossible to escape. If she made no marriage, she was doomed to a life of frustration. Not only was sexual satisfaction denied her but she felt herself branded a failure and must live on sufferance in the home of her parents, or of brother or sister, where she might have a meager emotional life from the love of other people's children. Not only must she suffer actual disappointment but she had the additional burden of inferiority feelings. She had failed to achieve the goal demanded by the culture—and for women there was only one goal.

Even in those days there were a few exceptions. For instance, the Brontes, although leading very frustrated lives, at least were able to develop their gifts and to achieve success. But work and the professions were for the most part closed to women. If one's own family could not provide for an unmarried woman, she might find a home as governess or teacher in some other family. However, there were occasional daring women. As early as 1850 a woman had "crashed" the medical profession. She was considered a freak and accused of immorality. She had to face insults and gibes from her colleagues. Very slowly the number of woman physicians increased. Still later, they entered the other professions and business. On the whole, the number of women who in one way or another became independent of their families before 1900 was small. The World War speeded the process and gave the stamp of social approval to economic independence for woman. Since then, she has been able to enter almost every field of work for which she is physically capable, but even yet she is seldom accepted on equal terms with men.

Interesting Factors in New Situation

Many interesting factors are revealed in this new situation of women. In the first place they are young in their present rôle. Comparatively few of them have the background of mothers or grandmothers who engaged in any work outside the home. They have to work out a new way of life with no precedent to follow and no adequate training from early childhood to help them take the work-drive seriously or fit it into their lives. It is not strange that the outstanding successes are few and that the great majority of women effect some compromise between the old and the new. For instance, the majority still plan to work only until they marry. This is true not only of the relatively unskilled worker but often of the highly trained. This may mean that the young woman not only does not do her pre-marital job well and in a way to give her satisfaction, but also nothing in her pre-marriage activity is helpful in fitting her for the business of homemaker.

Secondly, even when the individual has the courage in herself to attempt the new road, she has to cope with emotional pressures not only from society as a whole but from the individuals most important to her. One of the most significant of these pressures is the attitude of a prospective husband who has his own traditions and wishes for his future wife and, since he is often confused in his attempt to adjust to the new ways of life, may interpret the woman's struggle to find a place for herself as evidence of lack of love or a slur on his manhood.

Even the attitude of parents is often far from constructive. They do not have as great an emotional stake in a daughter's business success as in that of a son, and they are less likely to make sacrifices for her career. Sometimes they actually oppose it. For example: a young woman announced her wish to study medicine. Both parents disapproved and persuaded her to seek her career in music. She acceded to their wishes and spent several years in study. At the end of that time, she remained dissatisfied and again expressed her wish to study medicine. This time the parents persuaded her to take up nursing. When she had completed this course, she again asked to be allowed to study medicine and finally obtained her wish. She proved to have outstanding ability.

Because so much of the child's ideals is modeled on attitudes of the parents, the girl may be further handicapped by incongruities built into her own ego. For example, a young woman brought up in a southern home, where nothing was expected of woman except to be charming, found herself in adult life in a profession where she must compete to hold her own. Both healthy and neurotic factors had driven her from her parents adjustment. Her superior intelligence had stimulated her to go far in education, and lack of social ease—rising out of physical inferiority feelings—had reenforced this drive. Nevertheless, her ways of adjustment were definitely modeled on her past. Although she was in a position where she should be a leader with definite views and initiative to execute them, she was constantly deferring to men, seeking to flatter them by playing the yielding clinging vine, accepting their advice even when she thought differently. Her conscious desire to be a modern woman led her to pretend to herself that she did not want to marry. To prove it she had several extra-marital sexual affairs but in them she was frigid. She constantly felt humiliated because she had not achieved the traditional goal of marriage.

This example serves to show how the inconsistencies and conflicts—rising when a cultural situation is in a state of rapid transition—become a part of the neurotic conflict of the individual, even as they influence the form of the neurotic behavior.

Finally, social institutions put obstacles in the way of change of a woman's status. In the economic sphere she must usually accept a lower wage than men for the same type of work. She must usually be more capable than the man with whom she competes before she will be considered his equal.

Even with increased economic freedom, there is considerable variation in the social satisfactions available to independent women. In some groups any type of relationship with men or women is open to the woman who is emotionally able to accept it. In other groups a woman's social life may be even more restricted than it was in the days when she was overprotected in the home. In the latter groups, unless she shows great initiative in changing her situation, she may find herself forced to associate entirely with her own sex. While this is in itself a great cause for discontent, many individuals find a more or less satisfactory solution for its limitations, while others find neurotic security in the manless world. Thus it is possible for a woman teaching in a girls' school to reach the age of forty still living fairly happily on an adolescent "crush" level.

Whatever the problems created in the new life of woman, her status must continue to change for she is being driven out of the home by her restlessness due in part at least to her lack of occupation. The life of the married woman today who has no special work interest is not exciting. She has a small home, or in many cases only a small apartment. She may have no children; she may have at most three. Even if she does her own housework it is so simplified by modern inventions that it can fill only a few hours of her day. As has already been said, because of the nature of modern business life she often has very little share in her husband's interests. What can she do? She may make a cult of her child, or she may play bridge or have some other play life, or she may engage in some volunteer employment —in which she is apt to be no longer welcome since trained workers are increasingly preferred—or she may go to work seriously. The last solution is growing in popularity. (We must not forget that there still are women in this culture who function successfully according to the old stable pattern of the last century and contentedly manage their homes. These women need not concern us.)

Types of Reaction to Current Situation

Let us consider three frequently encountered types of reaction to the current situation: women who marry and try to live according to the old pattern but find themselves unemployed and often discontented; women who work and do not marry; and, women who marry and engage in serious work outside the home.

The first group, those who marry and have no other work interest, have already been discussed at some length. This is a very large group. It often happens that intelligent and capable women find themselves in this situation because they had not been aware of the reality before marriage and no preparation for any other type of life had been made. That is, these individuals had married with the phantasy that life after marriage could be lived somewhat in the old-fashioned way according to the pattern of the home life of their childhood. Many college women are in this group; especially college women who married immediately after graduation and did not fit themselves for any profession or work. Making a cult of the child is unfortunately a fairly frequent solution. By the term *cult* is here meant an anxious concern about the child's welfare where the mother goes to excessive lengths to apply all modern psychological and hygienic theories to the management of her child's development. This can be very destructive for the child.

Another type of woman finds in the marriage with no responsibility the fulfillment of her neurotic needs. This is the very infantile woman. For her, marriage is a kind of sanitarium life. She often shirks childbearing and in her relationship to her husband she has the position of spoiled child. Many of these women could not survive outside the protected atmosphere of their marriages.

Of the second group, those who work and do not marry,

there are two main subdivisions. First, there are those to whom work is everything; that is, there is no love life of significance. . . .

The second group are those who have a love life in addition to work. . . . The individual considers herself free although she actually may be very involved emotionally. She regards her work as the most important and permanent thing in her life.

In the group who marry and engage in work outside the home, several possibilities of relationship exist. Husband and wife may continue to lead independent business lives. They may be interested in each other's work without being competitive in any way. There may be real enjoyment in the success of the other. This is the ideal situation. It is more likely to work when the two are engaged in different types of occupation.

The husband's resentment and competitive attitude may crush the wife's initiative, a situation which was more frequent a few years ago. The man feels that his virility is threatened. He fears that people will think he can not support her or he fears that he will lose his power over her, and so forth. In such situations, if the marriage continues, the wife must give up her work—often without any interest adequate to take its place.

The wife who proves to be the better breadwinner may win out in the competition, especially since the depression. This is culturally a most revolutionary situation; it can make a great many difficulties. The woman needs extraordinary tact in handling it. If under the influence of her own cultural training she feels contempt for the husband or a desire to rub it in, matters can become very bad. In general, the man needs some face-saving explanation. He can not say that he prefers to keep house, even when, occasionally, this is the case. He could not accept it himself and most of his acquaintances would think less of him for it. So, he has to be unable to get work and, therefore, keeps house to help his wife who is working, or he must be ill, or he must be getting an education, in all of which cases he is able to accept his wife's economic support without loss of self-respect. . . .

Childbearing and Sexual Emancipation

Thus far we have said almost nothing about childbearing. What has become of this important biological function in our culture? In the present economic situation in the United States increase of population is not desired. The fact that small families are the rule is one of the factors driving women out of the home. Now that they are out of the home a kind of vicious circle is formed, for it is no longer convenient to be occupied in the home by one or two children. Much conflict centers here, for it is one of the problems of the culture which as yet has no generally satisfactory solution. Individual women have worked out ways of having both children and a career, but most women still do the one or the other; and in either case there are regrets and often neurotic discontent. The business or professional woman who had decided against children, consciously or unconsciously, does not want them; her difficulty arises from the fact that she often can not admit this to herself. Perhaps some biological yearning disturbs her, or some desire to have all of life's experiences, or perhaps there is merely the influence of the traditional cultural pattern which might be expressed thus: "A woman is expected to want a child." She may thus feel it her duty to prove her adequacy as a woman by having a child. She may resist, devote herself to her career, but it bothers her and makes her feel inferior. On the other hand, the problem is not solved by going to the other extreme and trying to prove one's adequacy as a woman by having a child or two. The women of past generations had no choice but to bear children. Since their lives were organized around this concept of duty, they seldom became aware of dislike of the situation, but there must have been many unwanted children then. Nowadays, when women have a choice, the illusion is to the effect that unwanted children are less common, but women still from neurotic compulsion bear children they can not love. It seems likely that the woman who really desires a child will find herself able to give it the necessary love, whether she devotes her life to its care or entrusts it to another while she is working. Since solutions to the practical difficulties are being found by way of day nurseries and nursery schools, it is probable that any woman with a genuine desire for motherhood can find a way in this culture today. . . .

A woman once needed . . . [marriage] as a means of economic support as well as a source of sexual satisfaction. Both factors have shrunk in importance. The companionship of marriage can conceivably be found in other situations; no satisfactory substitute has yet appeared to satisfy the economic and emotional needs of children. . . .

It is . . . apparent that while the sexual emancipation of women may be a step forward in personality development for some, it may only offer a new means for neurotic expression to others.

Overt homosexuality among women is probably more frequent at the present time than formerly. The diminishing emphasis on marriage and children helps to bring it to the fore, and the social isolation from men that now characterizes some types of work must be an encouragement to any homosexual tendencies which exist. It seems that many women who would otherwise never give overt expression to these tendencies are driven together by loneliness, and in their living together all degrees of intimacy are found. The culture seems to be decidedly more tolerant of these relationships between women than of similar ones between men.

Have the Changes Been Beneficial?

The question that is raised in any study of change, whether by evolution or revolution, takes the form: can one say that people are more benefited or harmed? Have our women actually solved any of their problems in the last fifty

years? When Freud analyzed his first cases, he described
some of the basic conflicts which we still encounter, albeit
the emphasis is different. Then, the young girl who might
wish to be a boy could only give symbolic expression to this
in the form of hysterical phantasies. Today, she may live
out the phantasy, at least in part. In her business relations
and in her sexual relations she may act in many ways like a
man. Many a woman with severe personality difficulties uses
the new opportunities provided by the culture for neurotic
purposes without much benefit except that in so doing she
is able to be a "going concern." On the other hand, many
women use the present-day situation more constructively.
As they acquire more freedom to express their capacities
and emotional needs, they find less actual reason to envy
the male. The handicap of being a woman is, culturally
speaking, not as great now as it was fifty years ago.

Inevitably, poorly adjusted people are in the vanguard
of revolutionary movements. This one for the emancipation
of women is certainly no exception. Women who studied
medicine in the early years were on the whole those who
had great personal problems about being women. Many a
parallel example readily comes to mind. Some therapists
may carry the marks of experience in those days. In any
case, there is a temptation to view all change as neurotic.
This obviously is an extreme stand. Neurotic drives often
find expression in the present-day activities of women but
this is no reason for dismissing as neurotic the whole social
and economic revolution of woman along her particular
path among the worldwide changes.

WHY MEN AND WOMEN THINK DIFFERENTLY [2]

It is currently fashionable to suggest that the commonly
observed differences in the intellectual capabilities of men
and women are determined by social conditioning rather

[2] From article by Kenneth Lamott, novelist and journalist. *Horizon.* 19:41-5.
My. '77. © 1977 by Kenneth Lamott. Reprinted by permission of the Harold
Matson Co., Inc.

than by biology. Our up-to-date conventional wisdom tells
us that intellectual ability is distributed by nature without
regard to sex. The comparatively low numbers of, say,
female engineers and mathematicians are taken as evidence
of the lack of encouragement and opportunity given to
women rather than any lack of particular abilities among
them. Yet within the past five years or so, a sizable body of
biological evidence has revived the ancient idea that the
brains of men and women are not identical but are specialized and intended to perform in somewhat different
ways.

The message that there are distinct differences of brain
organization between the sexes—biologically this is an example of dimorphism—is likely to be seized upon by the
fiercer feminists as one more attempt to deny woman her
rightful place in the world. But, as Corinne Hutt, a psychologist at the Human Development Research Unit at
Park Children's Hospital, Oxford, England, has remarked:
"The fact that such functional dimorphism exists may be
unacceptable to many human females, but denial of it
does not prove its absence."

The work currently under way tends to fall into three
fields of investigation: (1) the genetic transmission of certain abilities; (2) male/female differences in the development and functioning of the right and left hemispheres of
the brain; and (3) the influence of sex hormones on intellectual ability. . . .

These differences are necessarily determined by biology,
not by the environment, but as each child develops and is
shaped not only by his/her genetic heritage but also by
his/her experience of the world, the innate differences become obscured. However, we continue to recognize differences in the psychology of men and women regardless of
whether they have been shaped by biology or social conditioning.

In recent years a prodigious amount of scientific work
has been done in identifying psychological differences be-

tween men and women—in temperament, social behavior, and power relationships, as well as in general intelligence and capacity for achievement. Eleanor Emmons Maccoby, who heads the department of psychology at Stanford, and her colleague Carol Nagy Jacklin [undertook] to render this corpus of experimental work intelligible. . . . In the end Maccoby and Jacklin concluded that although there are some measurable differences in certain intellectual qualities of men and women, the differences are not at all large, and there is much overlap between the sexes.

Differences in intellectual quality do not necessarily imply differences in intelligence, of course. The argument as to whether men or women are on the whole more intelligent is doomed to remain unsettled for the good reason that nobody has managed to devise a generally acceptable definition of intelligence. . . .

Two substantial questions . . . must be tackled without flinching. First, are the differences that have been identified due entirely to social conditioning or are they dictated by differences in biology? Second, if these differences are indeed small, why is it that men have achieved so much more in doing the intellectual work of the world?

Biologically speaking, the essential difference between a man and a woman is that *she* started out with two X-chromosomes and *he* started out with an X-chromosome and a Y-chromosome. Everything else follows from this. The great question is whether differences in the quality of intelligence and in the ability to achieve intellectual work are transmitted with the chromosomes or are developed at home and at school. So far as the male's superior ability to solve spatial problems is concerned, there is good reason to believe that the answer lies in the chromosomes. . . .

The fact that women have not made large inroads into fields such as engineering, in which a high degree of spatial ability is needed, is clearly due to something more fundamental than the hostility of male engineers. It is due, in part at least, to biology. We must quickly remind ourselves that the difference is not of kind but of numbers. The women who are spatially gifted are fewer by half than the men, but the quality of their performance is just as high. So far as these individuals are concerned, the averages mean nothing at all.

Our understanding of the average male superiority in spatial thinking and the average female superiority in verbal fluency is strengthened by our growing knowledge about the development of the human brain.

One of the most distinctive features of the brain is that it is divided into two large hemispheres. Curiously, each hemisphere serves the opposite side of the body—the right ear, for example, reporting to the left hemisphere. In recent years, through the study of both normal people and the victims of brain damage, we have learned that the two hemispheres do not perform exactly the same functions. In right-handed people the left hemisphere is dominant for speech and the processing of information that is easily put into words, and the right hemisphere is dominant in the processing of spatial information and other material that is hard to put into words. In left-handed people the functions are reversed.

The specialization of hemispheres appears to develop differently in boys and girls. The lateralization of functions in one hemisphere or the other has been studied with regard to sex differences in both verbal and spatial performance. Doreen Kimura, an experimental psychologist at the University of Southern Ontario, suggests that dominance for speech perception advances more rapidly in the young female brain than in the young male brain. As for spatial ability, Sandra Witelson of the department of psychiatry of McMaster University, Ontario, reported in 1976 that her studies showed that the right hemispheres of boys had become specialized as early as age six, while this specialization was not found to occur with girls until age thirteen or later. . . .

From the evidence at hand it seems clear that a good

part of the difference in intellectual functioning of the
sexes has its beginnings in biology—in the different chro-
mosomal inheritances of men and women, in differences in
the lateralization of function in the two halves of the
brain, and in the influence of hormones on brain structure.
Without downgrading the part played by social conditioning, we are obliged to make room in our thinking for the
existence of innate differences in the brains of men and
women.

But what about the different achievement levels of men
on the whole and women on the whole? In recent years we
have all heard convincing arguments that men have generally been in charge and have prevented women from reaching positions of eminence and prestige. Many obstacles
surely did exist; since World War II we have seen them
being demolished one by one.

But what we have learned about the sexual dimorphism
of the human brain suggests strongly that women will
never be as numerous as men in engineering, architecture,
and most of the physical sciences. The same argument
turned around, however, suggests that women should be
pre-eminent in activities depending on verbal fluency, such
as literature and politics. It is true that women are well
represented in these fields, but not to the point of challenging male dominance.

Even after obstacles have been removed and even in
fields of their own choosing, women do not seem as aggressive as men in pursuing their goals. (In experimental psychology, aggressiveness is defined as behavior in which an
animal approaches a stimulus instead of fleeing from it.
This is roughly comparable to assertiveness in humans.) . . .

Social conditioning is suspect as the entire explanation,
since there are reasons for thinking that biology is at work
here, too.

Aggressiveness is a biologically determined trait that
is found more often in men than in women. Evidence of
male aggressiveness comes from anthropologists, etholo-

gists, and endocrinologists. It appears in virtually all human societies. The evidence of male aggressiveness in other mammals and in birds argues that it is not a characteristic of human society alone but a natural attribute of maleness. Finally, from studies with laboratory animals—rats, monkeys, and others—comes direct evidence that aggressiveness is influenced by the level of male hormones; that is, increased androgens result in increased aggressiveness.

Clearly, insofar as aggressive behavior is a desirable trait, the male animal has a considerable edge over the female, whether he is a white rat or a professor of the social sciences. And, as we have just seen, the hormones that control aggressiveness are also associated with levels of intelligence (or at least with high IQs). We are only beginning to make out the intricate patterns that are being woven by these influences on human behavior.

What are the principal implications of all this work? The female researchers themselves are in a unique position to tell us. Sandra Witelson believes that the differences between boys and girls in specialization of the brain's hemispheres may be critical when children are learning to read, and suggests that different methods of teaching reading may have to be adopted for boys and girls. The warfare between advocates of the "look-say" method and the phonetic method may have obscured the fact that one method may be better with boys and the other with girls.

Speaking to a scientific meeting in Paris in the fall of 1976, Eleanor Maccoby urged that no doors of opportunity be closed on the basis of findings about the different intellectual constitutions of the two sexes.

There is nothing we know about the psychological predisposition of the two sexes that would place any constraints on the ways in which women can adapt to their new opportunities [she said]. So far women have proved themselves capable of undertaking successfully a remarkable range of extrafamilial activities. The only way to be sure about what further modifications of male and female roles are viable is to try them out.

Doreen Kimura believes that biologically determined differences arose as adaptations during the evolutionary process. Corinne Hutt pursues the same theme in describing her own contribution:

There can be little doubt that these sex-typical patterns of abilities and behaviors are adaptive and, in evolutionary terms, have conferred distinct advantages. . . . To say this is not to discount the role of experience or learning, but it is as well for us to remember that experience acts on structure and machinery which is already biased to function in one particular direction. . . . Cultures and societies cannot create differences—they can only reflect and modulate those which already exist.

Now that it has been shown that there are sexual differences in what the genes transmit, in the hemispheres of the brain, and in the effects of hormones on the brain, we must also emphasize that these are average differences; they are of no use at all in predicting what a particular woman may accomplish in any field of activity. We accept this readily enough in the case of men and do not try to discourage young men from entering occupations in which female traits such as verbal fluency or persevering thinking are at a premium. Similarly, our new discoveries offer no argument at all for discouraging young women from becoming engineers or philosophers.

UNDERSTANDING
THE DIFFERENCE [3]

The first requirement for the acquisition of power by the Positive Woman is to understand the differences between men and women. Your outlook on life, your faith, your behavior, your potential for fulfillment, all are determined by the parameters of your original premise. The

Positive Woman starts with the assumption that the world is her oyster. She rejoices in the creative capability within her body and the power potential of her mind and spirit. She understands that men and women are different, and that those very differences provide the key to her success as a person and fulfillment as a woman.

The women's liberationist, on the other hand, is imprisoned by her own negative view of herself and of her place in the world around her. This view of women was most succinctly expressed in an advertisement designed by the principal women's liberationist organization, the National Organization for Women (NOW), and run in many magazines and newspapers and as spot announcements on many television stations. The advertisement showed a darling curlyheaded girl with the caption: "This healthy, normal baby has a handicap. She was born female."

This is the self-articulated, dog-in-the-manger, chip-on-the-shoulder, fundamental dogma of the women's liberation movement. Someone—it is not clear who, perhaps God, perhaps the "Establishment," perhaps a conspiracy of male chauvinist pigs—dealt women a foul blow by making them female. It becomes necessary, therefore, for women to agitate and demonstrate and hurl demands on society in order to wrest from an oppressive male-dominated social structure the status that has been wrongfully denied to women through the centuries.

By its very nature, therefore, the women's liberation movement precipitates a series of conflict situations—in the legislatures, in the courts, in the schools, in industry—with man targeted as the enemy. Confrontation replaces cooperation as the watchword of all relationships. Women and men become adversaries instead of partners.

The second dogma of the women's liberationists is that, of all the injustices perpetrated upon women through the centuries, the most oppressive is the cruel fact that women have babies and men do not. Within the confines of the women's liberationist ideology, therefore, the abolition of this overriding inequality of women becomes the primary goal. This goal must be achieved at any and all costs— to the woman herself, to the baby, to the family, and to society. Women must be made equal to men in their ability *not* to become pregnant and *not* to be expected to care for babies they may bring into the world.

This is why women's liberationists are compulsively involved in the drive to make abortion and child-care centers for all women, regardless of religion or income, both socially acceptable and government-financed. Former congresswoman Bella Abzug has defined the goal: "to enforce the constitutional right of females to terminate pregnancies that they do not wish to continue."

If man is targeted as the enemy, and the ultimate goal of women's liberation is independence from men and the avoidance of pregnancy and its consequences, then lesbianism is logically the highest form in the ritual of women's liberation. Many, such as Kate Millett, come to this conclusion, although many others do not.

The Positive Woman will never travel that dead-end road. It is self-evident to the Positive Woman that the female body with its baby-producinig organs was not designed by a conspiracy of men but by the Divine Architect of the human race. Those who think it is unfair that women have babies, whereas men cannot, will have to take up their complaint with God because no other power is capable of changing that fundamental fact. On some college campuses, I have been assured that other methods of reproduction will be developed. But most of us must deal with the real world rather than with the imagination of dreamers.

Another feature of the woman's natural role is the obvious fact that women can breast-feed babies and men cannot. This functional role was not imposed by conspiratorial males seeking to burden women with confining chores but must be recognized as part of the plan of the Divine Architect for the survival of the human race through the centuries and in the countries that know no pasteurization of milk or sterilization of bottles.

The Positive Woman looks upon her femaleness and her fertility as part of her purpose, her potential, and her power. She rejoices that she has a capability for creativity that men can never have.

The third basic dogma of the women's liberation movement is that there is no difference between male and female except the sex organs, and that all those physical, cognitive, and emotional differences you *think* are there, are merely the result of centuries of restraints imposed by a male-dominated society and sex-stereotyped schooling. The role imposed on women is, by definition, inferior, according to the women's liberationists.

The Positive Woman knows that, while there are some physical competitions in which women are better (and can command more money) than men, including those that put a premium on grace and beauty, such as figure skating, the superior physical strength of males over females in competitions of strength, speed, and short-term endurance is beyond rational dispute.

In the Olympic Games, women not only cannot win any medals in competition with men, the gulf between them is so great that they cannot even qualify for the contests with men. No amount of training from infancy can enable women to throw the discus as far as men, or to match men in push-ups or in lifting weights. In track and field events, individual male records surpass those of women by 10 to 20 percent.

Female swimmers today are beating Johnny Weissmuller's records, but today's male swimmers are better still. Christ Evert can never win a tennis match against Jimmy Connors. If we removed lady's tees from golf courses, women would be out of the game. Putting women in football or wrestling matches can only be an exercise in laughs.

The Olympic Games, whose rules require strict verification to ascertain that no male enters a female contest and, with his masculine advantage, unfairly captures a woman's medal, formerly insisted on a visual inspection of the contestants' bodies. Science, however, has discovered that men and women are so innately different physically that their maleness/femaleness can be conclusively established by means of a simple skin test of fully clothed persons.

If there is *anyone* who should oppose enforced sex-equality, it is the women athletes. Babe Didrikson, who played and defeated some of the great male athletes of her time, is unique in the history of sports.

If sex equality were enforced in professional sports, it would mean that men could enter the women's tournaments and win most of the money. Bobby Riggs has already threatened: "I think that men fifty-five years and over should be allowed to play women's tournaments—like the Virginia Slims. Everybody ought to know there's no sex after fifty-five anyway."

The Positive Woman remembers the essential validity of the old prayer: "Lord, give me the strength to change what I can change, the serenity to accept what I cannot change, and the wisdom to discern the difference." The women's liberationists are expending their time and energies erecting a make-believe world in which they hypothesize that *if* schooling were gender-free, and *if* the same money were spent on male and female sports programs, and *if* women were permitted to compete on equal terms, *then* they would prove themselves to be physically equal. Meanwhile, the Positive Woman has put the ineradicable physical differences into her mental computer, programmed her plan of action, and is already on the way to personal achievement.

Thus, while some militant women spend their time demanding more money for professional sports, ice skater Janet Lynn, a truly Positive Woman, quietly signed the most profitable financial contract in the history of women's athletics. It was not the strident demands of the women's liberationists that brought high prizes to women's tennis, but the discovery by sports promoters that beautiful female legs gracefully moving around the court made women's tennis a highly marketable television production to delight male audiences. . . .

Despite the claims of the women's liberation movement, there are countless physical differences between men and women. The female body is 50 to 60 percent water, the male 60 to 70 percent water, which explains why males can dilute alcohol better than women and delay its effect. The average woman is about 25 percent fatty tissue, while the male is 15 percent, making women more buoyant in water and able to swim with less effort. Males have a tendency to color blindness. Only 5 percent of persons who get gout are female. Boys are born bigger. Women live longer in most countries of the world, not only in the United States where we have a hard-driving competitive pace. Women excel in manual dexterity, verbal skills, and memory recall.

Arianna Stassinopoulos in her book *The Female Woman* has done a good job of spelling out the many specific physical differences that are so innate and so all-pervasive that "even if Women's Lib was given a hundred, a thousand, ten thousand years in which to eradicate *all* the differences between the sexes, it would still be an impossible undertaking. . . ."

Does the physical advantage of men doom women to a life of servility and subservience? The Positive Woman knows that she has a complementary advantage which is at least as great—and, in the hands of a skillful woman, far greater. The Divine Architect who gave men a superior strength to lift weights also gave women a different kind of superior strength.

The women's liberationists and their dupes who try to tell each other that the sexual drive of men and women is really the same, and that it is only societal restraints that inhibit women from an equal desire, an equal enjoyment, and an equal freedom from the consequences, are doomed to frustration forever. It just isn't so, and pretending cannot make it so. The differences are not a woman's weakness but her strength. . . .

The differences between men and women are also emotional and psychological. Without woman's innate maternal instinct, the human race would have died out centuries ago. There is nothing so helpless in all earthly life as the newborn infant. It will die within hours if not cared for. Even in the most primitive, uneducated societies, women have always cared for their newborn babies. They didn't need any schooling to teach them how. They didn't need any welfare workers to tell them it is their social obligation. Even in societies to whom such concepts as "ought," "social responsibility," and "compassion for the helpless" were unknown, mothers cared for their new babies.

Why? Because caring for a baby serves the natural maternal need of a woman. Although not nearly so total as the baby's need, the woman's need is nonetheless real.

The overriding psychological need of a woman is to love something alive. A baby fulfills this need in the lives of most women. If a baby is not available to fill that need, women search for a baby-substitute. This is the reason why women have traditionally gone into teaching and nursing careers. They are doing what comes naturally to the female psyche. The schoolchild or the patient of any age provides an outlet for a woman to express her natural maternal need.

This maternal need in women is the reason why mothers whose children have grown up and flown from the nest are sometimes cut loose from their psychological moorings. The maternal need in women can show itself in love for grandchildren, nieces, nephews, or even neighbors' children. The maternal need in some women has even manifested itself in an extraordinary affection lavished on a dog, a cat, or a parakeet.

This is not to say that every woman must have a baby in order to be fulfilled. But it is to say that fulfillment for most women involves expressing their natural maternal urge by loving and caring for someone.

The women's liberation movement complains that traditional stereotyped roles assume that women are "passive" and that men are "aggressive." The anomaly is that a woman's most fundamental emotional need is not passive at all, but active. A woman naturally seeks to love affirmatively and to show that love in an active way by caring for the object of her affections.

The Positive Woman finds somebody on whom she can lavish her maternal love so that it doesn't well up inside her and cause psychological frustrations. Surely no woman is so isolated by geography or insulated by spirit that she cannot find someone worthy of her maternal love. All persons, men and women, gain by sharing something of themselves with their fellow humans, but women profit most of all because it is part of their very nature.

One of the strangest quirks of women's liberationists is their complaint that societal restraints prevent men from crying in public or showing their emotions, but permit women to do so, and that therefore we should "liberate" men to enable them, too, to cry in public. The public display of fear, sorrow, anger, and irritation reveals a lack of self-discipline that should be avoided by the Positive Woman just as much as by the Positive Man. Maternal love, however, is not a weakness but a manifestation of strength and service, and it should be nurtured by the Positive Woman.

Most women's organizations, recognizing the preference of most women to avoid hard-driving competition, handle the matter of succession of officers by the device of a nominating committee. This eliminates the unpleasantness and the tension of a competitive confrontation every year or two. Many women's organizations customarily use a prayer attributed to Mary, Queen of Scots, which is an excellent analysis by a woman of women's faults:

> Keep us, O God, from pettiness; let us be large in thought, in word, in deed. Let us be done with fault-finding and leave off self-seeking. . . . Grant that we may realize it is the little things that create differences, that in the big things of life we are at one. . . .

Finally, women are different from men in dealing with the fundamentals of life itself. Men are philosophers, women are practical, and 'twas ever thus. Men may philosophize about how life began and where we are heading; women are concerned about feeding the kids today. No woman would ever, as Karl Marx did, spend years reading political philosophy in the British Museum while her child starved to death. Women don't take naturally to a search for the intangible and the abstract. The Positive Woman knows who she is and where she is going, and she will reach her goal because the longest journey starts with a very practical first step.

Amaury de Riencourt, in his book *Sex and Power in History*, shows that a successful society depends on a delicate balancing of different male and female factors, and that the women's liberation movement, which promotes unisexual values and androgyny, contains within it "a social and cultural death wish and the end of the civilization that endorses it."

One of the few scholarly works dealing with woman's role, *Sex and Power in History* synthesizes research from a variety of disciplines—sociology, biology, history, anthropology, religion, philosophy, and psychology. De Riencourt traces distinguishable types of women in different periods in history, from prehistoric to modern times. The "liberated" Roman matron, who is most similar to the present-day feminist, helped bring about the fall of Rome through her unnatural emulation of masculine qualities, which resulted in a large-scale breakdown of the family and ultimately of the empire.

De Riencourt examines the fundamental, inherent differences between men and women. He argues that man is the more aggressive, rational, mentally creative, analytical-minded sex because of his early biological role as hunter and provider. Woman, on the other hand, represents stability, flexibility, reliance on intuition, and harmony with nature, stemming from her procreative function.

Where man is discursive, logical, abstract, or philosophical, woman tends to be emotional, personal, practical, or mystical. Each set of qualities is vital and complements the other. Among the many differences explained in de Riencourt's book are the following:

> Women tend more toward conformity than men—which is why they often excel in such disciplines as spelling and punctuation where there is only one correct answer, determined by social authority. Higher intellectual activities, however, require a mental independence and power of abstraction that they usually lack, not to mention a certain form of aggressive boldness of the imagination which can only exist in a sex that is basically aggressive for biological reasons. . . .

De Riencourt provides impressive refutation of two of the basic errors of the women's liberation movement: (1) that there are no emotional or cognitive differences between the sexes, and (2) that women should strive to be like men.

A more colloquial way of expressing the de Riencourt conclusion that men are more analytical and women more personal and practical is in the different answers that one is likely to get to the question, "Where did you get that steak?" A man will reply, "At the corner market," or wherever he bought it. A woman will usually answer, "Why? What's the matter with it?"

An effort to eliminate the differences by social engineering or legislative or constitutional tinkering cannot succeed, which is fortunate, but social relationships and spiri-

tual values can be ruptured in the attempt. Thus the role
reversals being forced upon high school students, under
which guidance counselors urge reluctant girls to take
"shop" and boys to take "home economics," further confuse a generation already unsure about its identity. They
are as wrong as efforts to make a left-handed child right-
handed.

THE WAY
WE WERE—1949 [4]

In 1949 I was concentrating on breast-feeding and
wheeling Danny, my first baby, to the park, and reading
Dr. Spock. I was beginning to wonder if I really wanted
to go back to work, after all, when my maternity leave
was up. I bought a pressure cooker and *The Joy of Cooking* and a book by George Nelson about *The Modern
House*. One Saturday, though we had no money, we went
out to Rockland County and looked at old barns that my
husband might be able to convert into a house. And I
wrote my mother that I wanted the sterling silver—which
she had offered us as a wedding present and I had scorned
as too bourgeois—after all.

That was the year it really hit, the feminine mystique,
though at the time we didn't know what it was. . . .

After the war, I had been very political, very involved,
consciously radical. Not about women, for heaven's sake!
If you were a radical in 1949, you were concerned about
the Negroes, and the working class, and World War III,
and the Un-American Activities Committee and McCarthy
and loyalty oaths, and Communist splits and schisms, Russia, China and the UN, but you certainly didn't think
about being a woman, politically. It was only recently that
we had begun to think of ourselves as women at all. But

[4] Excerpts from *It Changed My Life: Writings on the Women's Movement*,
by Betty Friedan, writer, founder and past president of National Organization
for Women (NOW). Random House. '76. p 8-16. Copyright © 1974 by Betty
Friedan. Reprinted by permission of Random House, Inc.

that wasn't political—it was the opposite of politics. Eight months pregnant, I climbed up on a ladder on a street corner to give a speech for Henry Wallace. But in 1949 I was suddenly not that interested in political meetings.

Some of us had begun to go to Freudian analysts. Like the lady editor in Moss Hart's *Lady in the Dark,* we were supposedly discovering that what we really wanted was a man. Whatever the biological, psychosexual reality, a woman was hardly in a mood to argue with that message if (a) she was lonesome and tired of living alone, or (b) she was about to lose her job or (c) had become disillusioned with it. In 1949, nobody really had to tell a woman that she wanted a man, but the message certainly began bombarding us from all sides: domestic bliss had suddenly become chic, sophisticated, and whatever made you want to be a lady editor, police reporter, or political activist, could prevent or destroy that bliss—bourgeois security, no longer despised.

The magazines were full of articles like: "What's Wrong with American Women?"; "Let's Stop Blaming Mom"; "Shortage of Men?"; "Isn't a Woman's Place in the Home?"; "Women Aren't Men"; "What Women Can Learn from Mother Eve"; "Really a Man's World, Politics"; and "Nearly Half the Women in *Who's Who* are Single."

The short stories in those women's magazines we still read under the hair dryer were all about miserable girls with supposedly glamorous jobs in New York, who suddenly saw the light and went home to marry Henry. In "Honey, Don't You Cry" (*McCall's,* January 1949), the heroine is reading a letter from her mother: "You should come home, daughter. You can't be happy living alone like that." In "The Applause of Thousands" (*Ladies Home Journal,* March 1949), the young woman *pities* her poor mother who dreamed of being an actress; she is going to get married before she can even be tempted by such dreams.

I remember in particular the searing effect on me, who

once intended to be a psychologist, of a story in *McCall's* in December 1949, called "A Weekend With Daddy." A little girl who lives a lonely life with her mother, divorced, an intellectual know-it-all psychologist, goes to the country to spend a weekend with her father and his new wife, who is wholesome, happy, a good cook and gardener. And there is love and laughter and growing flowers and hot clams and a gourmet cheese omelet and square dancing, and she doesn't want to go home. But, pitying her poor mother typing away all by herself in the lonesome apartment, she keeps her guilty secret that from now on she will be living for the moments when she can escape to that dream house in the country where they know "what life is all about.". . .

In March 1949, the *Ladies' Home Journal* printed the prototype of the innumerable paeans to "Occupation: Housewife" that were to flood the women's magazines into the sixties. It began with a woman complaining that when she has to write "housewife" on the census blank, she gets an inferiority complex. ("When I write it I realize that here I am, a middle-aged woman, with a university education, and I've never made anything out of my life. I'm just a housewife.") Then the author of the reply, who somehow never is a housewife (in this case Dorothy Thompson, newspaperwoman, foreign correspondent, famous columnist), roars with laughter. The trouble with you, she scolds, is that you don't realize that you are expert in a dozen careers, simultaneously. "You might write: business manager, cook, nurse, chauffeur, dressmaker, interior decorator, accountant, caterer, teacher, private secretary—or just put down philanthropist. . . . All your life you have been giving away your energies, your skills, your talents, your services, for love." But still, the housewife complains, I'm nearly fifty and I've never done what I hoped to do in my youth—music. I've wasted my college education.

Ho-ho, laughs Miss Thompson, aren't your children musical because of you, and all those struggling years while

your husband was finishing his great work, didn't you keep
a charming house on $3,000 a year and paper the living
room yourself, and watch the market like a hawk for bar-
gains? And in time off, didn't you type and proofread your
husband's manuscripts, play piano duets with the children
to make practicing more fun, read their books in high
school to follow their study? "But all this vicarious living
—through others," the housewife sighs. "As vicarious as
Napoleon Bonaparte," Miss Thompson scoffs, "or a queen.
I simply refuse to share your self-pity. You are one of the
most successful women I know."

That year the *Ladies' Home Journal* serialized Margaret
Mead's *Male and Female,* with its deceptively tempting
version of a South Sea world where a woman succeeds and
is envied by men, just by "being" a woman. . . .

That year, the *Ladies' Home Journal* also serialized
Cheaper by the Dozen, the story of the lady engineer who
applied her scientific know-how to raising that newly fashionable large family. Very good reporters were given the
assignment of documenting in minute detail every detail
of the daily life of the newly glamorous American housewife—cooking in her own kitchen, with all her new appliances. It was also reported in the fall of 1949 that "something new in birth rates has occurred in the United States.
Between 1940 and 1947, the reproductive rate of women
college graduates increased 81 percent, compared with an
increase of only 29 percent among women who had completed only grade school."

It certainly did not occur to any of us then, even the
most radical, that companies which made a big profit sell-
ing us all those washing machines, dryers, freezers and second cars, were overselling us on the bliss of domesticity in
order to sell us more things. Even the most radical of us,
in our innocence, wanted those pressure cookers. . . .

"Security" was a big part of what began to happen in
1949. "Security," as in "risks," was in the headlines, as
in atomic secrets, Communist espionage, the House Un-

American Activities Committee, loyalty oaths, and the beginning of blacklists for writers. Was it unconscious political retreat that so many who had talked so bravely, and
marched, suddenly detoured to the security of the private
four walls of that house in suburbia—everything that was
"bourgeois." Suddenly we stopped using the word *bourgeois*. We were like our parents, it seemed. Suddenly we
were very interested in houses and *things:* chairs, tables,
silverware. We went to the Museum of Modern Art to
study furniture and displays of modern architecture, and
bought our first possessions—Eames chairs, a blond free-
form sculptured Noguchi dining table, and a Herman
Miller couch–daybed with a plain tweed-covered mattress
and bolsters, so modern, so different from the overstuffed,
tufted davenport at home (whose comfort I have now gone
back to.)

Toward the end of the year I read a story in the *Times*
about a new garden-apartment community in Queens
called Parkway Village, built for the UN with some va-
cancies for ex-GIs. It was almost like having your own
home: the apartments had French doors opening on to a
common lawn where the children could go out and play
by themselves, instead of having to be taken to the park.
And there was a cooperative nursery school. During my
lunch hour I took the subway to the wilds of Queens, and
so began the fifteen-year trek of my own particular nuclear
family away from the city, to that garden apartment in
Queens, to a rented barn in Sneden's Landing, to our own
eleven-room Charles Addams Victorian house in Rockland
County, where my children (increased to three) grew up,
and I chauffeured, and did the PTA and buffet dinners,
and hid, like secret drinking in the morning, the book I
was writing when my suburban neighbors came for coffee,
The Feminine Mystique.

I felt that I would never again, ever, be so happy as I
was living in Queens. The floors were parquet, and the
ceilings were molded white plaster, no pipes, and the

plumbing worked. The rent was $118.50 a month, for four and one half rooms, and we thought that was enormous. And now our friends were the other couples like us, with kids at the nursery school who squealed at each other from the baskets of the grocery carts we wheeled at the supermarket. It was fun at first, shopping in those new supermarkets. And we bought barbecue grills, and made dips out of sour cream and dried onion soup to serve with potato chips, while our husbands made the martinis as dry as in the city and cooked hamburgers on the charcoal, and we sat in canvas chairs on our terrace and thought how beautiful our children looked, playing in the twilight, and how lucky we all were, and that it would last forever.

There were six families in our group, and if your child smashed his finger in the manhole cover and you weren't home, one of the others would take him to the doctor. We had Thanksgiving and Christmas and Passover Seders as a joint family, and in the summer rented houses together, on Lake George and Fire Island, that we couldn't afford separately. And the support we gave each other hid the cracks in our own marriages—or maybe kept them from getting serious. As it is, of the six families, three couples are now divorced, one broken by suicide.

Having babies, the Care and Feeding of Children according to Doctor Spock, began to structure our lives. It took the place of politics. But the mystique was something else—that college graduates should make a *Career* of motherhood, not just one or two babies, but four, five, six. Why even go to college?

I remember the zeal with which we took the classes at the Maternity Center. Our husbands were envious, but then with natural childbirth the husbands could take the classes too, and breathe along, and show off at dinner parties, doing the exercises on the floor. And then there was the moral, political seriousness of our breast-feeding. In the summer of '49, I was frowned on for breast-feeding in public, on the front steps of my husband's summer theater.

It wasn't fashionable then. But it's so *natural,* we gloried, feeling only scorn for our superficial selfish sisters who thought breast-feeding was animal and would spoil their figures. (Actually, I did not breast-feed in public—I'd retire to the back row of the darkened theater where they were rehearsing. But I did sit out on the front steps afterwards, burping him in the sun.) And how proud I was, continuing the breast-feeding nearly all that year, even after the milk began to give out and I had to sterilize bottles anyway. And how furious I was, when they called from the office and insisted I come back to work, one month before that year's maternity leave was over, because it was messing up vacation schedules.

So twenty-five years later when that grown-up boy is having trouble with his girl, and—knowing Freudian words himself, if not yet Dr. Spock—says his insecurity in love is all my fault, I still feel the pains of the guilt caused by leaving my first baby with a nurse when I went back to work. Would all that guilt have been necessary if Dr. Spock hadn't said, in the section on "Should Mother Work?":

> In most cases, the mother is the best one to give him this feeling of "belonging," safety and security. . . . If a mother realizes clearly how vital this kind of care is to a small child, it may make it easier for her to decide that the extra money she might earn, or the satisfaction she might receive from an outside job, is not so important after all.

To be honest, those years were not all products of the "mystique." I still remember the marvelous dark night in the spring of 1949 when we were wheeling Danny home in the baby carriage. I looked down as we passed under a streetlight, and he was smiling at me, and there was recognition in his eyes. A person was there, and he knew me.

Besides, the reality of the babies, the bottles, the cooking, the diapering, the burping, the carriage-wheeling, the pressure cooker, the barbecue, the playground, and doing-it-yourself was more comfortable, more safe, secure, and satisfying—that year and for a lot of years thereafter—than that supposedly glamorous "career" where you somehow didn't feel wanted, and where no matter what you did you knew you weren't going to get anywhere. There was a guilty feeling, too: it was somehow your fault, *pushy* of you, to want that good assignment for yourself, want the credit, the by-line, if the idea, even the writing, had been yours. *Pushy,* too, if you felt rejected when the men went out to lunch and talked shop in one of those bars where women were not allowed—even if one of those same men asked you out to lunch, alone, in the other kind of restaurant, and held your hand, or knee, under the tablecloth. It was uncomfortable, unreal in a way, working in that kind of office with "career" still driving you, but having no words to deal with, even *recognize,* that barrier that you could never somehow break through, that made you invisible as a person, that made them not take you seriously, that made you feel so basically unimportant, almost unnecessary, and—buried very deep—so angry.

At home, you *were* necessary, you were important, you were the boss, in fact—the mother—and the new mystique gave it the rationale of career.

The concrete, palpable actuality of the carpentry and cooking you could do yourself, and the surprising effectiveness of the changes you could make happen in school boards and zoning and community politics, were somehow more real and secure than the schizophrenic and even dangerous politics of the world revolution whose vanguard we used to fancy ourselves. The revolution was obviously not going to *happen* that way in America by 1949: the working class wanted those pressure cookers, too. It was disillusioning, to say the least, to see what was happening in the trade unions, and in Czechoslovakia and the Soviet Union, even if the myth of the Communist menace was mostly an excuse for red-baiting. In 1949, McCarthyism, the danger of war against Russia and of fascism in America, and the reality of US imperial, corporate wealth and power all made men and women who used to have large visions of making the whole world over uncomfortable with the Old Left rhetoric of revolution.

Suburbia, exurbia, with the children as an excuse—there was a comfortable small world you could really do something about, politically: the children's homework, even the new math, compared to the atomic bomb.

The feminine mystique made it easier for a woman to retreat smugly, without the pangs of conscience and self-contempt a man might feel while using all his wits to sell cigarettes that would cause cancer, or deodorants. We could be virtuous and pure of compromise, and even feel a smug contempt for the poor man who could not so easily escape the ulcerous necessity of really conforming and competing. For a long while, it looked as if women had gotten the better of that bargain. It was only later that some of us discovered that maybe we had walked as willing victims into a comfortable concentration camp.

Shortly after 1949, I was fired from my job because I was pregnant again. They weren't about to put up with the inconvenience of another year's maternity leave, even though I was *entitled* to it under my union contract. It was unfair, *wrong* somehow to fire me just because I was pregnant, and to hire a man instead. I even tried calling a meeting of the people in the union where I worked. It was the first personal stirring of my own feminism, I guess. But the other women were just embarrassed, and the men uncomprehending. It was my own fault, getting pregnant again, a *personal* matter, not something you should take to the union. There was no word in 1949 for "sex discrimination."

Besides, it was almost a relief; I had begun to feel so guilty working, and I really wasn't getting anywhere in that job. I was more than ready to embrace the feminine mystique. I took a cooking course and started studying the suburban real-estate ads. And the next time the census taker came around, I was living in that old Charles Addams house we were fixing up, on the Hudson River in Rockland County. And the children numbered three. When the census taker asked my occupation, I said self-consciously, virtuously, with only the faintest stirrings of protest from that part of me I'd turned my back on—"housewife."

A CULTURAL DILEMMA [5]

I use the title "A Cultural Dilemma" because I feel that what is happening at present is not nearly as much a question of legislation alone or of organized prejudice alone, as it is a question of the way in which our society itself is organized.

If one goes back to the beginning of women's suffrage in this country—and as a small child I used to accompany my mother on women's suffrage demonstrations. I even learned to recite a monologue which caricatured anti-suffragettes who I grew up to believe were very fast, wicked, rich women with poodle dogs; so that I have in a sense been acquainted with part of the women's movement in this country ever since I was a small child.

But it is not that the legal barriers in this country against women are so serious, although there are some serious ones, and there are states that discriminate against women in giving them greater punishment. There are enormous degrees of discrimination in marriage laws and property laws, and there are a great many legislative deficiencies that ought to be wiped out. But the essential thing that has happened in this country is that we have nominally

[5] Address entitled "Women's Rights: A Cultural Dilemma" delivered to the Conference on Women's Role in Contemporary Society, New York City, 1970, by Dr. Margaret Mead, anthropologist and writer. *In* New York City Commission on Human Rights. Women's Role in Contemporary Society; Report, Sept. 21-25, 1970. Avon Books. '72. p 172-83.

given women freedom to act as individuals, as human beings, as men are allowed to act most of the time, but we haven't given it to them *in fact*.

We have a style of life which discriminates against the way in which women can live; discriminates, on the one hand, against the married woman with children who must, if she wants to have the marriage and have children, undertake an enterprise which is too much for her if she tries to make a contribution to society as well as to her own home. This is for the married woman. Or, on the other hand, she can become a spinster and accept all the social disabilities of spinsterhood, which include the failure of society to recognize that most spinsters have relatives to support and aged mothers that they are not allowed to take overseas, and things of this sort.

I have been asked to review briefly the way in which the position of women today is related to their position in the past, and I will try to do that in as few words as possible.

I do not subscribe to the general popular position that men oppress women, and that women's position should be against men as being one vast conspiracy against their becoming people, because I have lived too long and worked too closely with women in different stages of civilization to accept this kind of version of society.

In every society in the world, with occasional very brief exceptions, the society has been worried for fear that they would not have enough children, that their numbers would decrease, their strength would decrease, and their particular style of life, whether it was religious or nationalistic or simply a small group of people in New Guinea, would vanish.

When a people are afraid that their population will go down and that they will suffer, it is necessary for them to use every inducement they can to make men and women spend their time having children and bringing them up. I think it is very important to emphasize that through history men have also spent their time on the next generation—not only women.

But the society has been organized to make young people want to marry, want to have children, to make the woman want to stay at home and look after them, and make the man want to work and toil to support his children so that there will be another generation. This has been true everywhere in the world. Contrary to the mythologies that are sometimes advanced, there has never been a society dominated by women, and there has never been a society where women played a more important public role than men. There have, of course, been queens, but the point about a queen is simply that genealogy has temporarily been regarded as more important than sex, but not for the bulk of the population.

For the first time in history it is to the interests of no society to have a great number of children and a rising population. This is new. It is something that has never happened before in the history of the world, something that is due to the way our world is organized today.

And so for the first time in history society can afford not to release just a few women and a few men—I want to emphasize it is only a few men who have ever been released—from the daily round of caring for the next generation. We now can afford to release large numbers of people for most of their lives, some people for all of their lives, from the problems of child production and parenthood.

This has come about, of course, because with our modern medicine we can save and rear almost every child that is born. It has also come about because with our modern electronic revolution in the world we no longer need millions of hands to do the work that can now be done by machines.

So what we need is a higher quality of human beings, fewer children, better brought up, better cared for, better educated, and that means that we don't need more parents. But we do need more of every other kind of expert person who cares for children—more pediatricians, better teachers, all the way along the line—because each child to be educated up to the standard that is needed in a modern society needs more and more adult time.

This means we are releasing both men and women from the continued grind of child care all their lives to perform all of these other services that society needs. Of course, this is associated with a change in public attitude toward all of the methods of population control. We have seen very marked and unexpected change in the attitude toward abortion in many states in this country and around the world today. Whereas abortion was vigorously opposed in most societies, and will, I think, again be opposed as a desirable method of population control, today people, realizing the extremity of the situation, are beginning to remove legislative impediments, and societies are financing and approving research on population control and research on the spread in education of the people toward the control of population and the use of contraceptives.

All of these go together. They are not, I believe, accidental. They are all related to the period in which we live. When it is possible for societies to say to women, "You need not marry; you need not have children; you can have only a few children; we will reward you if you don't have too many children, and we will give you help in bringing up those children," this is all of a different order from anything that society has ever been able to do before.

I believe that the present renewed interest in the status of women in this country began with President Kennedy's Commission on the Rights of Women—but it was very peculiar at that period because that Commission report only discussed the working woman and her disabilities, which are extreme. She is badly paid. She has access to lower-level jobs.

What women do in this country compares very, very unfavorably with what they do, for instance, in the Soviet Union. We don't have more women working than they do. They don't have more women working than we do. But they have a much larger number of women working at high-level tasks than we do. Our women are underachievers. Their women, I think, in many cases are overachievers, because they lost so many men in the war; whereas we did not lose an enormous number of men in World War II. When they came back from the war, women who had achieved a great competency and efficiency were described as "over-mature" and "over-experienced" and very delicately pushed out of the jobs that they had done very well at during the war in many instances.

What has happened today is primarily a precursor of the world to come, a precursor of the fact that we will look forward to people having no more than two children, that we will be working for zero population growth, and that we must construct a world that fits this kind of population growth, instead of the kind of population growth that has been favored in the past. (As so many children died, it was necessary for so many people to spend their entire lives having children.) This means that we are not going to be able or willing to support women all their lives in return for having between the ages of eighteen and twenty-two had two children.

In the discussions of the *oppression* of women that are so popular today, we forget the fact that in the past societies have also *supported* women. For a very long time they supported all women—either husbands or brothers or fathers or sons being expected to give women economic security, such as they had available for them. Women were expected to receive this in return for fulfilling a domestic and parental role. Of course, most of them died young, which made it a great deal easier. One of the other conditions today, which puts us in the dilemma that we are in, is that women live so long. It is one of the complications of marriage for life because marriage for life used to mean marriage for a rather short period. The more children your wife had, the more likely she was to die young and could be replaced by another young woman, who could have some more children, so that the really vigorous men might send three or four

women down to the graveyard with a lot of children to their
credit. Vigorous women sometimes married two and three
husbands because the period of life was so short. The expectation of life was so short. Today when a woman of twenty
marries she has to look forward to something like fifty-five
years ahead.

If she is to earn her place in the community, earn her
right to respect, earn her right to a share in the economy, to
a dignified secure place in her society, she can't earn that in
the few years she has two children and brings them up. She
has to have also a right to work in some way and contribute
to the wider society.

But we have set up a style of life—here I return to the
question of lifestyle as being the important thing at present
—we have set up a lifestyle that makes this exceedingly difficult. We have let our cities deteriorate, so that almost every
responsible young couple, as soon as they have children,
flees to the suburbs. In the suburbs we have created the sort
of situation where there is one class economically and very
often one religious group, where there are highly segregated
groups, where there is no one to help with anything. There
are many suburbs where even retired bank executives can't
afford to live, so their successors in the bank have to look
after their own children because there aren't even grandparents around to look after them.

We have created a situation where the care of children
goes on in such isolation that no woman without extraordinary energy, cooperation from her husband and luck can
hope to be able to care for small children and make any
substantial contribution to what is going on. I hope all
these different qualifications are heard. She has got to have
extra energy, she has got to have extra imagination, and she
has got to have luck; otherwise it is almost impossible.

And so what we have been doing in the last fifty years is
creating a society where we have educated women—up to a
point. Of course, the proportion of women in graduate
school is smaller than it was thirty years ago. But we put

them through college or halfway through college. We have given them a reasonably good expectation of being people, and we have then refused them the opportunity to use those skills in that background which they attained with an education, where they might have expected that they would have an opportunity to be people, as well as to be mothers and housekeepers.

At the same time we have done something which I think is relevant to the interest of this Commission [New York City Commission on Human Rights]. It is a very peculiar operation. We have denigrated every form of domestic work. Then we have taken our most highly educated and most fortunate women and locked them up at home with a vacuum cleaner. If you have a two-story house, you get two vacuum cleaners, one for upstairs and one for downstairs, to save you steps. Then you go to work to make a little more money to pay for the vacuum cleaners.

But, we have locked them up in the suburbs at the same time that we have so denigrated the work they are doing, which is described as "slavery" and "association with little people under two feet high," and other forms of horror, that no woman on the whole, even though she needs work, is willing to work as a domestic either in caring for children or in cooking or cleaning the house.

This is something where both things have to be changed. We have to reorganize society so that there are services available, drop-in day care centers, day care centers for women who work, day care centers for women working part time who need a place to park their children temporarily, resources so that we do not have millions of women staying home for a week waiting for the man from the telephone company who doesn't come or the plumber to come and fix something.

We are making the most uneconomical use of highly educated time that we possibly could. This is the life of the average woman in the suburbs: Even if the children are in school, she has to stay home for a week because there must be someone to answer the door while somebody comes to take away all the things she bought that are necessary, all of which are imperfect and need to be returned to the manufacturers for adjustment.

We have created then a lifestyle which penalizes intelligence, which prevents those women who would have gladly, even though they themselves are not married at the moment or don't have some spoiled children, spend their time in homemaking if it were not denigrated, if it had not been discriminated against in provision of legislation for a very long time. It is not unionized. We have no dignity or protection for the women who will care for children while other women who are trained for special activity do the other things that they need to do.

Unless, then, we change our style and make adequate provision for homemaking being associated with other contributions and for homemaking being dignified, something to be treated with respect, something to be adequately paid for, we have very little hope, no matter how much legislation we pass, of changing the position of women in the United States.

We can improve a great deal by legislation. We can improve the income tax adjustment. We can set standards . . . [dealing with] employers who discriminate against women— and they do discriminate against women—because the women are trying to do an impossible task, and no matter how well they attempt to do it, the children do get the measles.

There are those, of course, who advocate that you pass some kind of legislation that permits fathers to stay home when the children have the measles. I think this is simply imperiling and impoverishing the rest of the population. We would do much better to change the style, the institutional style, in which we live.

We have no reason to believe on the basis of cross cultural and historical study that women are less able to undertake any order of task than men. Person for person men are stronger than women physically, but there is hardly anything that is done today with exercise of real strength. It is all done with buttons, and women are just as good at pushing buttons as men are.

Women have forms of endurance that men don't have. Men have forms of spurts of energy possibly that women don't have. We are not even certain that that is true because it is possible for society to reverse it. But there is some suggestion that it may be true.

Women traditionally in the past were physiologically vulnerable. They were vulnerable during adolescence. We used to have a tremendous death rate of young girls. Some of you may remember Beth in *Little Women*. But young girls don't die today from consumption as they did then. We used to have a considerable amount of periodic instability in women, which we can iron out very easily today with modern medical methods.

As far as we can tell, women have a period of extra excess of energy, a postmenopausal zest, which could be used very effectively for society, but is largely used today in making their husbands miserable.

I think one of the reasons for the large amount of middle-aged postparental divorce in this country is the disparity between men who have reached the heights of their careers and want to go fishing and women who feel they haven't done anything yet and would like to start.

This is a very uncomfortable kind of household in many instances, and we should allow both for the period of young womanhood, when many women would like to bring up their own children and be dignified for doing so and helped to do so, and also for the period after the children are grown when women have this extra freedom and extra zest, which they could contribute to the community if the community were so organized that they could do so.

I would like to stress very strongly that I am not advocating that we send every woman to work, nor am I advocating, as I was misquoted in the press a few months ago, when

I wrote an article for *Manpower,* that all women return home.

I am advocating that we should have a society that permits a young couple to see that their children have excellent care. That excellent care can be provided by the mother, by the father, by grandparents, by adequately trained professional people who can give their time to it. But we do know children need continuity of personal care.

The only continuity of personal care that this society respects at present is breast feeding mothers. If the mother is not breast feeding her baby, they put it in the hospital nursery and lock her out. The only way in which you can really be sure that you have some relationship to your baby is to breast feed it, even if you don't have much food. It doesn't really matter because society still thinks that they can't take a breast feeding baby away from its mother. And so at present I am advocating that everybody breast feed.

But at present we have no provision that really respects a mother and child tie, and we have no provision whatsoever that provides continuity of care for young children. Yet we know that, and we have very adequate and carefully controlled studies, such as those made by Renée Spitz, that point out the disastrous effects on infants of separation from whoever is giving them continuity in their lives. If the mother is to make some other contribution to society, then some other member of the household or the neighborhood must provide that continuity.

I think that the position that was taken by the President's Commission [on the Rights of Women], which had a few polite sentences about motherhood in it, where it said, after discussing at great length all the difficulties of the working woman—and they are manifold and plenty—it then said, "Nothing should interfere with her discharge of her duties as wife and mother," as if they were something she did five minutes every day.

I think the emphasis that some of the more extreme members of the women's liberation movement have placed on abortion and day care centers is nevertheless very important because the emphasis on abortion, which gives women a right over their own fertility, treats them as whole human beings who control their own bodies and their own autonomy: and the emphasis on day care centers, which emphasizes the importance of institutional change—I think these are both exceedingly important and symbolize the problems that are facing us in this country today.

II. CHILDHOOD AND EDUCATION

EDITOR'S INTRODUCTION

How much do girls and boys really differ in infancy, in early childhood, and during primary school years? For centuries, it has been assumed that there are vast differences between the sexes beginning at birth: biology is destiny. This has been asserted, believed, and documented in many different ways with the result that boys and girls have been given vastly different treatment from day of birth. Recently, however, there has been a shift in the thinking of some educators, psychologists, and various nonprofessionals, including parents, to the view that it is the difference in treatment that *causes* many differences thought to be biological. This sex-role conditioning affects personality traits, specific kinds of intellectual and emotional capabilities, and future professional potential.

The articles in this section are concerned with various aspects of early and secondary education in areas relating to sex-role conditioning. Barbara Grizzuti Harrison discusses preschool children and the question of "appropriate" toys for them. Gurney Williams III next deals with the dispute over coeducational sports in elementary and high schools. There follows a selection of editorial comments on the problems raised by federal regulations banning sex discrimination in schools. Opposition to school programs based on the regulations is expressed by the conservative writer Russell Kirk and by a clinical psychologist, Dr. Rhoda L. Lorand, both of whom uphold traditional roles and denounce "unisex education" as unwise and unsound. The next article discusses the results of nationwide achievement tests and offers some possible explanations of why girls lag on tests. In the concluding article in the section Robert J.

Trotter considers the possibility of altering or eliminating, through school programs and training, sexist attitudes heretofore fostered in children.

EARLY STEREOTYPES [1]

> Sugar and spice and everything nice,
> That's what little girls are made of.
> Frogs and snails and puppy dog tails,
> That's what little boys are made of.

> Freedom does not alter the innate
> predilection of the sexes.—A. S. Neil

> A little girl is treated and molded
> differently from a little boy from the
> day she is born.—Benjamin Spock

To offer the complexities of life as an excuse for not addressing oneself to the simpler, more manageable (trivial) aspects of daily existence is a perversity often indulged in by artists, husbands, intellectuals—and critics of the women's movement. When feminists focus their attention on the liberation of their children from sex-role stereotypes they often begin at the beginning; they begin, that is, with blocks and dolls. And immediately they are accused of busying themselves unproductively with trivia. (The same charge, however, is seldom leveled against radical therapists whose patients begin at the beginning by reenacting their blocks-and-dolls childhood.) Feminists are loftily called upon to justify their concern with blocks and dolls; they might just as well be asked to justify Freud's dictum that what happens in the nursery asserts itself in the man. People whose lives are messy and confused, painful and unmanageably complex—and who hope that their children's lives will be better, will be golden and joyous and filled with clarity and delight

---

[1] Excerpt from *Unlearning the Lie: Sexism in School,* by Barbara Grizzuti Harrison, free-lance writer, member of Parents Committee on Sexism at Woodward School in New York City. Liveright. '73. p 1-11. Copyright © 1973 by Barbara Grizzuti Harrison. Reprinted by permission of Liveright Publishing Corporation.

—often disdain talk of blocks and dolls. . . . *Trivia!* But they are wrong. Novelist Joan Didion was wrong when, in her important essay on the women's movement, she pointed to feminists' concern with "a nursery school where the little girls huddled in a 'doll corner' and were forcibly restrained from playing with building blocks" as evidence that the basic philosophy of feminism had been trivialized. Didion spoke for many when she questioned what blocks and dolls have to do with the "irreconcilable difference" of being a woman, "that sense of living one's deepest life underwater, that dark involvement with blood and birth and death." But dolls and blocks do have a great deal to do with that sense of *otherness,* with the "irreconcilable difference" of being a woman. Revolt and adventure are not paths open to girls; women sense that men have a direct and purposeful connection with the world, while they exist only in connection with men. Keeping girls in the doll corner, while boys are zipping around, moving, thrusting, making splashy changes in their environment, molding their world, helps to foster an *artificial* difference, a difference which is perceived, by women, as a lack, and called, by men, "inferiority." (Perhaps there are *innate* irreconcilable differences other than the obvious biological ones. But how, huddled in our separate corner, with no psychic room to exercise free choice, are we to know that is so?) Girls spend all their young lives playing with dolls, obsessed with domestic relations, and they grow up needy and wanting and waiting (for a man), obsessed, to the point of madness, with their relationships with their men and their children. It is thrilling to read about the obsessions and the madness, but it is terrible to live with the obsessions and the madness. Some of us celebrate our pain in poetry; it falls to others to do something about the culture that produced the madness. No one wishes to deny the blood and birth and death that are part of our lives; but most of us, while living our "deepest lives underwater," have occasionally to come up for air—to go to the supermarket, or the orthodontist, or to pick the kids up from their (sexist) schools. (Even poets take time off from their magical lives to go to the laundry—unless, of course, their wives do it for them.) Nobody claims that by rearranging blocks and dolls feminists hope to create a stark new political-poster world in which ironies and moral ambiguities will not exist. What we say is that we will, hopefully, give our boys and our girls a better way to deal with moral ambiguities, ironies, and despair, by not cruelly limiting the ways they may choose to deal with them.

So, to begin at the (not so trivial) beginning, with blocks and dolls, sugar and spice, snails and puppy dog tails:

In Gesell and Ilg's classic behavioral guide, *The Child from Five to Ten,* there is a rather remarkable sentence: "At two and a half years of age," these experts state, "boys may prefer girls' toys." But, one might reasonably ask, if boys are naturally drawn at an early age to dolls, dollhouses, and housekeeping equipment, what justification exists for calling them *girls'* toys? Gesell and Ilg provide the answer: "The child is taught by suggestion and indirection."

What the child is taught, in fact, is that girls will be (and damn well better be) girls, and that boys will be (and damn well better be) boys. They have to be *carefully* taught; if they are not, say Gesell and Ilg somewhat skittishly, "something unexpected is likely to occur."

As long as we respected the advice of gurus like Dr. Spock, there was small chance that "something unexpected" would occur:

If I had a daughter, I'd dress her in clothes that were different from boys'. If she asked to wear blue jeans like her brother, I'd tell her how much I like to see her looking nice in girls' clothes. When I found her fighting with her brother over a truck that I knew she never paid any attention to when he was away, I'd remind her firmly that she has much more fun with her girls' playthings. Because young girls have a readiness to believe unconsciously that their mothers have not endowed them as well as boys, they need lots of evidence that their mothers enjoy them just because they are girls, just because they can shop together, talk about babies, clothes and interior decoration.

While the belief that they are inadequately endowed may be unconscious, the programming for that belief is overt, if not calculated. To the question, "Why don't I have a penis like Johnnie?" many of us have considered "Girls don't have penises" an appropriate response. Suppose we had said, "You have a womb, breasts, and a clitoris, and Johnnie doesn't"? Would our daughters then have felt underendowed? (It's interesting, by the way, that Spock chooses to project blame on the *mother* for what's supposedly missing from girls. It would be even more interesting to know if he also assigns her the credit for the superior endowment of boys.)

These are the toys Spock exhorted parents to buy for boys: cars, trucks, buses, trains ("partly because they are symbols of masculinity, and also because of the variety of ways and levels in which they can be used"), model cars, planes, trains, boats (because they develop, "not only manual skill, interest in mechanics, and a sense of history, but also basic creativity"), woodworking tools, building sets, and construction sets.

These, he said, must be girls' playthings: dolls, dolls' clothes and equipment, housekeeping equipment, dolls' cribs, prams, bureaus, china and cutlery; child-sized stoves, refrigerators, dining tables, laundry equipment; needle-work sets, and bead-stringing sets. These goodies, he said, would inspire girls to "play out . . . dramas of parent-child relationships, friendships, school life, adventure, romance, domestic existence." (In all fairness, he does list one androgynous plaything: a bicycle.)

Dr. Spock claims to have changed his thinking since 1955, when he pooh-poohed "the women called feminists, who are resentful of men's advantages." If he has, the producers of television commercials have not. Trucks are invariably advertised as "boys' toys" (as are war toys, or anything that smacks of dominance or aggression); and you don't catch a boy on the television saying "Look, ma! she walks, she talks, she cries, she wets!"

One wonders about the little boy who, perversely, after the two-and-a-half-year-old magic cut-off time, still wants to play with a doll. "Conscious of the excessive cultural pressure exerted by the disapproval of his parents," say Gesell and Ilg, he believes he is "not orthodox; so he keeps his doll somewhat out of sight." . . . A small boy once went to the pathetic extreme of fashioning a stuffed airplane to take to bed to "cuddle," thus, presumably, preserving his orthodox masculine image while satisfying his need to nurture and to gentle.

And what of the little girl who learns—earlier than boys do, according to Gesell and Ilg—her "assigned sex role" (a role which, according to these theorists ,"is progressing toward marriage")? If she is not entirely pleased with her vast array of Lilliputian domestic playthings, she might do what one . . . child was observed to do—push her carriage around with a dump truck in it. That *is* unorthodox.

We are told, by the psychologists who insist on innate temperamental differences between boys and girls—the very same psychologists who dictate what toys boys must have and what toys girls must have—that a three-year-old boy, asked "Are you a little boy or a little girl?" is likely to respond, "No, I am a *big* boy." A three-year-old girl asked the same question is likely to reply, "I'm a boy." Well, no wonder. While a boy is "developing manual skill, an interest in mechanics, a sense of history, and basic creativity," a girl is playing with tiny tea cups. Tiny tea cups pall.

And why, after all, can't a boy "play out . . . dramas of parent-child relationships, friendships, school life, adventure, romance, domestic existence"? Why, indeed! What are we doing to our children?

We are destroying their spontaneity—and therefore, in large part, their joy. We are telling them, "by suggestion and indirection" what is good for them. We are—with benevolent intent but malevolent consequences—assigning them roles based on gender without regard to their individual natures and their needs.

Having done this scrupulously from the moment of their birth (just think how you would have reacted if your baby boy had been wrapped in a pink blanket), we then pronounce, as if it were God's own truth, *"Boys will be boys, girls will be girls."* Or, if we are psychologists or educators, we dress up the bromide to sound really heavy and authentic:

"It's a great mistake to try to minimize [temperamental differences] in any way." (Spock)

"To what extent the manifold differences are due to a cultural bias the statistics do not disclose. The bias itself must have been originally produced by innate differences in the sexes. In any event, the end result is that each sex tends to play the role assigned to it." (Gesell and Ilg)

"Freedom does not alter the innate predilection of the sexes." (A. S. Neil)

No parent sets out to be wicked. The man I saw at the zoo cafeteria who told his little boy to "sit in the blue chair because you're a boy" probably didn't even hear himself say it (although, as a matter of fact, he said it three times, and one wonders whose masculinity was being insisted upon, and how many "symbols of masculinity" are necessary before a boy can assert his "innate temperamental difference"). If a feminist had told this father that what he was doing was part of a whole network of messages perceived and assimilated by his child that would have consequences in the way the boy would one day understand and act in the world (not to mention in bed, in his work, with his mother, with other women, with lovers, and with men), he would have thought her mad. Yet the messages are daily and unremitting. They are trivial, perhaps, in each instance, but taken cumulatively, they articulate a world-view; they tell our children what it is to be a male human being, and what it is to be a female human being.

So it is not carping, and it is not a preoccupation with

trivia, to ask if we are not programming our children from the time they are given to us to guide and protect, in ways that are designed to limit and contain them in the strait-jacket of gender-based roles. "Little" things can have big repercussions, as Spock *et al.* foresaw when they implored us to slap a little girl's wrist if she presumed to play with symbols of masculinity.

For example:

A fire engine rushes past your house. Whom do you call to see it? Your daughter, or your son?

You drive past a wedding party. Whose attention do you call to it? Your son's, or your daughter's?

You are given flowers. Whom do you ask to arrange them prettily in a vase? Your son, or your daughter?

Out walking with your children, you pass a woman with a small baby. With whom do you share your pleasure in the infant? Your son, or your daughter?

A building is under construction. To whom do you point out the crane, the workers, the details of construction? Your daughter or your son?

Relatives come to visit. Do they hug and kiss your daughter and tell her how pretty she looks? Do they shake hands with your son, toss him up in the air, and jocularly mess up his hair? Why?

Your small son asks for a doll, a toy oven, or a jump rope. How do you react?

Your daughter and your son both ask for trucks for Christmas. Who gets the 29-cent truck in the Christmas stocking? Who gets the $9.95 truck under the tree?

Would a stranger be able to tell the sex of each of your children from their respective Christmas lists?

(I gave my daughter a dollhouse this past Christmas; it was what her heart desired. My son's heart desired a football, binoculars, and a pedometer. Like many feminists I know, I am not unwilling to give my children "stereotypical" toys when they are expressly wished for. I see the charm and the magic of a dollhouse—a manageable world—myself. I would reproach myself, however, if all of Anna's toys were "feminine," and if, on the other hand, Josh got all the active-adventure-doing stuff. . . . When Josh—who is ten—was four, he very much admired a girl-playmate's dollhouse—though he confided to me his intention of hiding any dollhouse under his bed that he might be lucky enough to get. I didn't ever give him one—and now I can't think of a single reason, aside from unreasonable fear and prejudice, why I did not. . I think it's important to see children in a continuum. Last year, for example, Anna—who is nine—wanted science kits and a camera; she scorned dolls as much as she now takes pleasure in dollhouses. . . . What I'm suggesting is not that parents issue a hammer to a kid who wants a teddy bear, or a Raggedy Ann to a kid who wants a baseball mitt, but that—*from the earliest age*—we expose all our children to the widest possible variety of playthings, and that we begin to look at many more playthings as androgynous and appropriate to either sex.)

Look at your children's books. In how many is the main character (animal or human) male? In how many is the main character female?

Would you be inclined to give your son a book in which the leading personality was a girl? How many books does your daughter have in which the leading personality is a boy?

How often have you heard parents say: Boys don't cry. Girls shouldn't fight. Be a man, son. Be a lady, honey. Boys will be boys. Girls will be girls.

Your daughter is called a tomboy. Your son is

called a sissy. How, in each case, do you react? To
which description do you react more negatively?
Have you thought about why?

("Sissy," I think, would undoubtedly scare the hell out of
most parents, while "tomboy" would do little more than
produce a tolerant smile; and for the same reasons that
parents are much more inclined to be fearful of their boys
becoming homosexual than their girls. We unconsciously
seem to value maleness so much more than we do femaleness: to be a tomboy is, one might say, to be upwardly
mobile, while to be a sissy is to ape a despised sex. Considering that men implore women to be "feminine," but jeer
at them for being female, it's not surprising that a "feminine" male is very bad news. I think also, that we assume
girls will "grow out" of tomboyishness—there is evidence
that girls "settle down" to their assigned roles earlier than
boys do; trained to be docile and dependent, they know it's
in their best survival interests to do so—we make no such
assumptions about "sissies." Perhaps the explanation is
even simpler: we just never take girls—or their sexuality—
seriously.)

And the result: while "four- and five-year-old children
often play the role of the opposite sex, . . . by the age of
seven, the shifting in roles becomes less frequent." In other
words, by the time they're seven, they know what's "orthodox," they know what's good for them, they know what's
culturally sanctioned, and they know that their choices are
limited by their gender. By "playing the role of the opposite sex," one is not to understand Gesell and Ilg to mean
anything as titillating as precocious sexual play. What they
mean is "many a four-year-old boy has asked for a doll for
Christmas." Why that should be *opposite* to his sex, in
view of the fact that Gesell and Ilg themselves say it is
normal, is not quite clear. They admit that most four-year-

olds behave like this, yet they say that such behavior is inappropriate to their sex. The mind boggles.

All of us, children and adults, parents and educators, have learned our lessons well. So well that by the time our rigorously groomed children reach school, this is what we are likely to find . . . :

Teachers expectations of girls are different from their expectations of boys: A number of kindergarten children are working at a carpentry bench. A girl shows her teacher (male) her handiwork. "These nails aren't hammered in far enough," he says, "I'll do it for you." A boy shows the teacher his handiwork. "These nails aren't hammered in far enough," the teacher says. "Take the hammer and pound them in all the way."

The Cinderella Syndrome: (dialogue in a second-grade classroom), six-year-old Mary to student teacher: "Johnnie hates me." Student teacher: "Of course he doesn't hate you. How could anybody hate such a sweet, pretty girl?" Mary: "Oh, yes, he hates me. Ask him." Student teacher to John: "You don't hate Mary, do you?" John: "Yeah, I hate her." Student teacher: "How could you hate anybody so pretty?"

Boys are expected to be physically aggressive: A sixth-grade class trip to an ice-skating rink; a boy pushes and shoves a girl, who, falling, retaliates by calling him a four-letter word. A concessionaire who has witnessed the incident later refuses to serve the girl, because "ladies don't talk like that." The girl, irate, complains to the school's director; the director, sympathetic to the girl's feeling of having been messed over, nevertheless counsels her to have "a decent respect for the opinions of others," and suggests that the sensibilities of a hot-dog vendor who is appalled by a girl's using street language have got to be taken into consideration. Somehow the initial provocation—the boy's physical aggression—is overlooked in the discussion of the girl's verbal response.

Styles differ according to sex: Boys erect massive block structures; girls tend to build nesty, small-scale constructions. A nursery-school teacher takes a radio apart. The boys rush over, clamoring to see how it works, while the girls, happily festooning one another with the laces and cast-off jewelry of the costume box, stay put. Boys are mobilized by the opportunity of seeing how things function. Girls seem content to engage in passive, ornamental activities.

Girls relate to esthetics; boys relate to scientific principles: A group of first- and second-grade children is in the playground, observing clouds. The boys discuss the movement of the clouds, the wind, the power that pushes them across the sky. The girls say, "Oooh, aren't they pretty?"

Sex-role stereotyping is unquestioned: Eighth-graders discuss *The Grapes of Wrath.* A young girl, asked to define the qualities of Steinbeck's characters, says, "Rose of Sharon is completely obsessed with her pregnancy. That's what she's about." "Ma," says a boy, "gets it all together. The family couldn't make it without her." "Apple-pie mother," interjects another boy, with a laugh that is rather sly. "No, not really," corrects the teacher. "Steinbeck sees woman as earthmother, as a pillar of strength, nurturing, supportive. . . ." "Right! Apple-pie mother," says one of the girls.

When boys violate girls' physical integrity, the girls are held equally to blame: Embarrassed third-grade girls complain of boys "pinching their bottoms" and of boys peering over lavatory walls to "spy on them." The teacher suggests to the girls that they were "teasing" the boys, and to the parents that the girls were being "provocative." A parent questions her girl: "Mommy, I was teasing, I guess. But I don't know what I *did.* I don't know *how* I teased. I never touched *them.*" *When girls are assaulted, they feel guilty.*

Incidents like these are the stuff education is made of. And the programming and the attitudes that give rise to incidents like these are also reflected in a school's curriculum, in a version of history that centers—literally—around *man's* development, in textbooks, in readers, and in physical activities. Our children are not learning to be their best selves; they are learning what society—male-dominated society—requires females to be, and what society requires males to be.

How do we change the pattern? How do we unlearn the lie that girls are innately passive, unaggressive, supportive, and domestic; that their nature is to need, and to want, and to wait, while boys are innately dominant, achieving, adventurous, and aggressive, their nature to seek and to dominate? How do we free our children to choose their own styles, their own lives, their own pleasures, and their own work? How can we reverse sexist indoctrination so that powerful people of *either* sex may exercise their right to power without having to dissemble, manipulate, pretend, destroy others or themselves in the process? How can we make it possible for nurturing, compassionate people of *either* sex to delight in their own natures without fear of scorn? What is required to make our children fully human, fully aware of all the options available to them? How do we free them to avail themselves of the human privilege of taking their own risks in their own time, and in accordance with their own singular natures regardless of gender?

BOYS, GIRLS, AND SPORTS [2]

It's a heated match. The sides are racing toward the extremes. One team argues females will bust their bones, batter their psyches, or—the ball is going! going!—wreck marriage prospects with bulging muscles. The other team chants "Chauvinism!" as they rush headlong into a condi-

[2] Article entitled "Superbowl Time in the Battle of the Sexes," by Gurney Williams III, free-lance writer. *Science Digest.* 77:10-15. Ja. '75. Reprinted with permission of *Science Digest.* Copyright © 1975 The Hearst Corporation.

tioned line, bursting for gains in sports games long ago set aside by sane men.

It's Superbowl time in the battle of the sexes. The battle-grounds are playing fields, pools, rivers and courts, and the weapons of choice are tennis rackets, bats, footballs, oars and pucks. Zing! The number of girls participating in high school sports jumps 175 percentage points in two years. Splash! The Yale swim team adds a coed diver to its roster, drowning a 122-year-old tradition of male-only competition. Blam! In Dallas, one hundred girls show up to try on gloves—boxing gloves to punch their way to the Missy Junior Gloves title.

And in California, a little boy feels guilty when he recalls the time he made that beautiful slide into second—and knocked the female baseman flat.

The story of women and sports goes back as far as Callipateira, a mother in ancient Greece, who trained her son to be a runner. The Greeks were champs in chauvinism: Their women weren't even allowed to *watch* sports. To watch her son compete, Callipateira dressed up like a man and sneaked through the gate, risking the unsubtle punishment of being hurled from a cliff. She later gave herself away by screeching while her son competed, but authorities decided to let her live and allow other women to watch sports as well. The result—after a couple of millennia—was Billie Jean King.

So heated has the competition become today that an august, all-male committee of the American Medical Association issued a "special communication" last summer [1974], a pronouncement many will take as the rules of the game between sexes.

The six doctors tried manfully to put women in their place albeit a somewhat *higher* place than old-fashioned doctors once assigned them. At one time, a report in the *Journal* of the American Medical Association said, "female participation (in sports) was discouraged due to societal and cultural stereotypes that considered such participation a departure from the 'traditional role.' " Now, however, it's clear that females on the field stand to win "physiological and social benefits," and even improve their "distinctive biological functions."

But the committee also issued a caveat or two, causing a few feminists to counter with a Callipateiran screech.

☐ In general, the committee argued, boys and girls ought to try out for sex-segregated teams, since, after puberty, "only the exceptional girl will have the necessary ability to make and compete on a boys' team."

If girls try out for boys' teams, boys will inevitably try out for girls' teams and take all the top slots, the committee said.

☐ Contact sports between girls is trickier to call because of the risk of fractures. There's not much scientific data to help. Ladies do suffer more fractures than men on ski slopes, but part of that can be blamed on gravity. Theoretically, the committee said, there's no reason why girls can't play football or ice hockey *with each other:* "The lesser muscle mass of girls makes it unlikely that they would experience as many fractures as do boys."

☐ But football between boys and girls? It's not safe, the committee said, even if lineman is matched by weight with linewoman. The reason is that a greater percentage of a woman's body is fat, 25 percent compared to a man's 15 percent in one study, and that means men have more muscle, pound for pound, than women.

Couldn't the extra padding on women offer a kind of protective shield? It's possible, said Dr. Timothy T. Craig, one member of the panel responsible for the report. "Fat does seem to offer protection," he said, "but there haven't been any studies comparing fracture rates of men, for instance, with those of women of the same weight in sports like football." Hence, based on physiological assumption, weight for weight, women can't generate the same muscle force as men and are therefore more likely to get punched around or have sand thrown in their faces if they insist on competing with men in some sports.

Feminists generally don't argue with the facts of the AMA report. Craig got only one letter from a woman objecting to the part about how "distinctive biological functions" are improved by exercise. Her point was that doctors wouldn't feel compelled to argue that football, say, improves the sexual functioning of men. Craig's response: nobody's ever charged that male sports impair a man's "distinctive biological functions."

But feminists do argue against some of the recommendations. And they suggest that the reason women are generally also-rans in the race with men is that society *wants* them to be. "So now they acknowledge that sports and even contact sports are healthy for girls and women," said Joan Goldstein, a former assistant professor of sociology at Brooklyn College. "Only a few years ago, they were saying sports increased the severity of menstrual cramps. It's too bad we didn't hear all this before." She said the AMA report reflected a cultural lag in the medical profession, supporting limited contact between the sexes just when women had become ready to challenge every male on the field.

"When I was growing up," she said, "the only acceptable physical activity for young women was dancing, and I got strong doing it, masked behind ruffled skirts and pink shoes." Now she regularly plays tennis with men. "But it's funny. Sometimes when I play a reasonably good game, I notice this irritation from the man on the other side of the net. He'll say something like, 'You're making me run all over the court.' We can be more active now, but we're still not supposed to win."

Can women win against men? Yes, some scientists suggest, challenging the weaker-sex label traditionally slapped on women. "This stigma may be just another culturally induced myth," said Dr. Jack H. Wilmore, associate professor of physical education at the University of California.

"Today, we're starting to look at [female] subjects who are more fit and better trained." Rigging the training odds slightly begins to even the score between the sexes.

In one recent study, two groups of nonathletic people —one group male, the other female—began a physical fitness program in California. After ten weeks of slinging weights around, the women had improved their strength, as measured by how much tension they could apply to a spring as well as by how much weight they could lift, by a full 30 percent. The men improved too, but proportionally not as much. Wilmore also took initial measurements of the leg strength of his groups. He found that men's legs were 25 percent stronger than women's.

But, and here's where the figure fiddling comes in, when the strengths were expressed relative to body weight, the difference between men and women shrank to 7.6 percent. And when strengths were expressed relative to the estimated weight of the muscle itself, women came out 5.8 percent *stronger,* strength that Wilmore suggests may be buried under cultural prohibitions.

Craig said female journalists spring the culture question on him all the time. "They always push me to the point of answering the question, 'Aren't women as good as men? And if not, isn't that a result of culture?' I tell them I still think women have a distinct and different biological function. All of a sudden the door's open; women are saying 'We're as strong as men. We want to compete all over the place.' To me it's like a man saying, 'I can give birth to a baby.' It's just not there, fella."

Females are more physically advanced than males during one glorious time in their junior high years, when they're about twelve. Their greater height and weight and bone maturation, compared with boys of that age, is an enormously complicating backdrop to the debate on whether girls should play Little League baseball (ages nine–twelve) with boys. The dust has settled somewhat, now that the national board of the Little League voted unanimously last June [1974] to let girls try out. But before that vote, the question had reached courtrooms in ten states, including California, New York and Michigan. The sexual world series had already begun.

The contenders chucked scientific studies around like fast balls. Dr. Creighton J. Hale for one, executive vice president for Little League, argued that female bones are more susceptible to fracture than males'. Opponents countered by pointing out that studies cited by Hale involved strength tests on the bones of deceased adults, and that it was unfair to extrapolate from cadaver bone to child bone. Since girls are more advanced than boys at age twelve, their bones may actually be stronger, anyhow.

Hale: Girls don't react as fast as boys, as a study shows.
Opponents: The boys in the study cited were 7.3 years old on average; the girls were only 5.4 years old. That's an apples-vs.-oranges argument.
Hale: The muscle mass of males puts females at a disadvantage; they'll be hurt.
Opponents: Muscle strength doesn't become significant until about age thirteen. Besides, most sports injuries result from falling down or twisting limbs, not from collision.

Psychiatrists entered the fray, too. "There have been no really proven, established tests showing that mixing boys and girls in sports is harmful from a *physical* standpoint," said Dr. Thomas Johnson, a California psychiatrist, and consultant to a number of pro-football teams. "But from a psychological standpoint, it has the potential of being harmful." Children of Little League age, he argued, need a variety of activities, including adult-supervised, structured play both sex-integrated and separate-but-equal. For one thing, separate recreation provides a forum, he said, for girls to discuss mutual concerns, such as breast development and the onset of menstruation. Integrated sports can be confusing "at a time of critical importance for children trying to sort themselves out.

"One little boy injured a girl playing second base at a school picnic," said Dr. Johnson. "Some of his friends remarked, 'What's the idea of sliding into a girl?' Others said, 'Attaboy! You really gave it to her good!' The boy was terribly confused. On the one hand, he felt pleased to have the opportunity to smash into the girl; on the other, he felt guilty about the feeling.

"As another example, let's say a boy tackles a girl in a football game. There's a good possibility he'd be sexually stimulated by that, and the stimulation could create a confusing feeling."

Right, agreed Dr. Carol Nadelson, assistant professor of psychiatry at Harvard. But single-sex sport can be just as sexually stimulating to youngsters of that age, who often go through a homosexual phase before settling into heterosexual roles. She also agreed with Johnson that junior high youths need private peer groups from time to time, in part to talk about what's happening to their bodies.

"But I think we're dealing with a larger issue that may be analogous to the school discrimination issue. You can go on saying people are happy living apart, separate but equal, but there are other issues." Children themselves may have the final say on those issues, Nadelson said.

"I asked my next door neighbor, who is a boy, how he would feel having a girl on his Little League team and his first question was 'Is she good?' I said, 'Yeah,' and he said, 'Okay.' The fact is, boys and girls are pushed toward alienation from each other."

But what happens after Little League? It seems clear that some sex-integrated sports are unsafe for women now, but women could go much further, and science can help.

One way was suggested by Katherine Ley, a professor at the College at Cortland of the State University of New York. She said researchers could boost the safety of contact sports between sexes by developing an overall physical rating system for every child, beginning in elementary schools. A formula for each child's rating would swallow weighted data on characteristics such as age, weight, speed and strength. Then the formula would crank out a number that would be used to assign children—and eventually older participants as well—to teams of competitors with similar numbers.

Girls' numbers would probably be higher than boys' during several of the junior high school years. But then, she said, "I suspect we'd find boys' numbers would surge ahead again. We might find a point at which there is so great a difference between boys and girls that gym classes, for instance, should be separated by sex."

As male-female competition increases, suggested Dr. Clayton Thomas of Tampax Inc. and a consultant on human reproduction at the Harvard School of Public Health, there are even more fundamental questions that must be asked: Are some sports even unsafe for males? And are some just plain dangerous to human beings? "Male testicles, for instance, are much more at risk than female breasts, and much more important in a way, because a lady could have her breasts severely damaged and still bear children, but a man who loses his testicles can't father them.

"I don't think people should catch cannon balls," Thomas said. "And I don't like to see wrestlers covered with mud or people competing by butting their heads together until one passes out, or dueling with candles on a powder keg. But if men are silly enough to do it, is it fair to prevent women?"

SEX BIAS IN SCHOOLS [3]

The Ford Administration June 3 [1975] sent to Congress new federal rules prohibiting sex discrimination in schools.

[3] From *Editorials on File.* 6:641+. Je. 1-15, '75. Reprinted with permission from *Editorials on File.* © 1975 Facts on File, Inc.

. . . Elementary schools are given a year to comply and high schools and colleges up to three years. The regulations seek to offer equal opportunities for women in the areas of faculty hiring, admissions, financial aid, vocational and academic counseling, and athletics.

Among the present practices to be abolished are hiring on the basis of marital status, suspensions from classes of pregnant students, sex quotas in medical and law schools, sports scholarships for men only, and separate curfews for men and women. Physical education classes are to be integrated, but contact sports can be separate. Any sport offered to men must be available to women if there is sufficient interest. Separate home economics and industrial arts classes are forbidden.

The regulations were issued under Title IX of the Educational Amendments of 1972 which prohibited sex bias in educational programs. Health, Education, and Welfare Secretary Caspar W. Weinberger estimated that the rules could apply to approximately 16,000 public school districts and 2,700 colleges and universities receiving federal aid.

The Providence Journal

(Editorial June 8, 1975, Providence, R.I.)
Reprinted by permission of the Providence Journal Bulletin.

The Ford Administration, in announcing long-awaited regulations dealing with sex discrimination in the nation's schools, has taken an important step toward strengthening the concept of equal opportunity for women. Ironically, as it was codifying provisions for equal treatment of the sexes, the Administration disclosed a new policy widely interpreted as a step backward in the enforcement field.

The Department of Health, Education, and Welfare has proposed an end to its investigation of individual complaints. Instead, it would concentrate on patterns of discrimination that develop on an institutional basis—at schools and colleges and industries that receive federal aid, for example. In this way, HEW officials believe they can utilize the federal team of about five hundred inspectors nationwide more effectively.

Indeed, there is something to be said for the broader approach. If an entire industry were brought into compliance by this means, the results could be far more productive on a per capita basis and as an example to others than if each of several thousand complaints were handled individually. The drawback, however, is that the aggrieved citizen's only options may be to tolerate unjust treatment silently or file legal action in the courts.

Complaints from women have increased over the last three years since Title IX of the Educational Amendments of 1972 was passed. Title IX prohibits discrimination against women in 16,000 public school systems and 2,700 colleges, universities and graduate schools on peril of losing federal funds. The new regulations designed to implement the law are likely to increase the number of protests from women who believe they are the victims of bias.

The new rules bar unequal treatment in the areas of school admissions, employment, financial aid, vocational and academic counseling and athletics. The last mentioned promises to stir the greatest controversy because it requires fundamental changes in traditional attitudes and practices. While sexually integrated athletic and physical education programs are mandated, colleges are given three years in which to adjust their policies and procedures. Even then, flexibility appears to characterize the administrative approach. Said HEW Secretary Caspar W. Weinberger, his department is not looking for hard rules to lay down but for colleges to show "good faith" that they will comply with the law.

There are bound to be rough spots ahead, particularly in the athletic transition. Sports at the campus level have been male-dominated so long that equalizing attention to women's activities—balancing scholarship aid, providing

coaching staffs that are equivalent in terms of quality, and
making facilities, equipment and travel allowances comparable—is certain to encounter obstacles large and small.

One point beyond questioning is that educational inequality between the sexes long has been subject to comprehensive overhaul. Simple fairness demands that women
not be limited to second-class status. Understandable, perhaps, are the fears of college administrators and coaches
that the highly profitable men's intercollegiate competition
will suffer erosion. But that assumes no corresponding increase in the popularity of women's competition. An estimated 60,000 women enrolled in collegiate sports last year
[1974], twice the number in 1972 and four times the figure
for 1967.

Title IX doubtless is seen as a threat by many American males who prize the traditions of the athletic field and
fear the shifting balance of physical prowess once considered a typically male attribute. But an evening of the score
is both necessary and inevitable in all areas covered by
the new rules. While the athletic dispute may well stimu-
late the most adrenalin, it is not sports but equal opportunity to obtain an education that lies at the heart of the
matter.

The Salt Lake Tribune

(Editorial, June 5, 1975, Salt Lake City)

An attempt to be reasonable is apparent in the United
States Department of Health, Education, and Welfare's
latest rule-making against discrimination. But that hasn't
insulated the agency from revived criticism.

After hearings, deliberations and revisions, HEW has
produced its final draft of regulations implementing federal law prohibiting discrimination in the country's school
systems based on sex. Since so many schools and higher education institutions depend on federal money, the rules will

compel change, but as compromise, the law interpretations still displease those taking extreme positions on the issue.

To its credit, HEW did modify earlier proposed requirements, allowing schools to provide equal but separate programs or facilities for boys and girls, men and women where this distinction made obvious sense. Previously, it appeared the government would order fully integrated activities in every instance, whether this included classroom instruction, choral groups, living accommodations or competitive athletics. Now, the department stresses it expects only equal opportunities among the sexes, students and faculty, which should avoid ridiculous lengths to which preliminary regulations could have driven school programs. It won't, however, stop the pressuring.

Women activists are already angry because the rules don't cover references in textbooks which stereotype male-female roles. The department answers this would have made it a "federal censor." The women critics, nonetheless, have at least one legitimate beef.

Along with the rules, HEW announced it would no longer investigate every sex discrimination complaint the department gets. Rather, the agency is giving schools a chance to reverse sex discrimination during a "good faith" period. Since the law requires complaints be investigated within ninety days after being made, HEW may have no authority to arbitrarily drop the procedure.

Living up to the rules even as they've been promulgated won't be easy in every case. School administrators around the nation, although not in Utah, are complaining that equal facilities and opportunities, especially for interscholastic sports, will be prohibitively costly. A spokesman for the National Collegiate Athletic Association warned: "This may signal the end of intercollegiate athletic programs as we have known them in recent decades." Which may not be quite as doleful as it's made to sound. Still, it would be wrong to destroy men's athletic programs with strict rules setting up equivalent opportunity for a female participation that never actually materializes.

In essence, HEW has built a set of guidelines having expansion joints, something mandating change, but not immediate, complete alteration. This is the practical, rational approach. More rule revisions may be necessary, reflecting actual experience, but, conscientiously applied, the new regulations should help displace mistaken concepts fostering discrimination based on sex. That, after all, is the purpose of the legislation and the interest behind it.

UNISEX AND THE PUBLIC SCHOOLS [4]

Unisex marches on. Early in June [1975] the federal bureaucracy, in the name of Mr. Gerald Ford and Mr. Caspar Weinberger, Secretary of the Department of Health, Education, and Welfare, conferred upon us a document of fifty-four small-print columns entitled "Nondiscrimination on Basis of Sex: Education Programs and Activities Receiving or Benefiting from Federal Financial Assistance." These are regulations compelling educational institutions which receive federal funds to treat girls as if they were boys and boys as if they were girls.

Immediately after issuing this ukase, Secretary Weinberger resigned his secretaryship and fled to California. President Ford has expressed no contrition for promulgating these decrees from the throne, but he may yet be sorry. Congress can undo these requirements, quite as Congress undid the seatbelt interlock system. Already, encouraged by howls from constituents, Congress has postponed for a year execution of these new rules.

This federal document, however, is not nearly so extreme as the anti-feminine feminists, or libbers, would like.

[4] From article by Russell Kirk, noted author and scholar. *National Review*. 27:887. Ag. 15, '75. Reprinted by permission of *National Review*, 150 E. 35th St., New York, NY 10016. ($19 per year)

It grants certain exemptions and stops short of censoring textbooks (at the federal level, anyway) for "sexist bias." Aye, reaction as yet has not been wholly stamped out at HEW: paragraph 86.61 actually admits that in rare circumstances the authorities may recognize "sex as a bonafide occupational qualification": chiefly, it is not forbidden to consider "an employee's sex in relation to employment in a locker room or toilet facility used only by members of one sex." Tories!

The follies of this HEW manifesto have been widely criticized already. Many people are unaware, however, of the yet sillier antics of certain "Sex Bias Task Forces" which are endeavoring to bully departments of public instruction and public schools in the several states. I have at hand information about such Women's Lib pressure in Minnesota and Michigan; had I time, doubtless I could make a collection of similar propaganda materials from other states. Early this year a "Sex Bias Task Force" delivered a report to the Minnesota State Board of Education, and just before the federal decree was published, the "Task Force to Study Sexism in Michigan Schools" presented a similar report to the Michigan State Board of Education.

In Michigan, three dissenters from the strident Report (all of them women) protested against the arbitrary methods and extreme conclusions of the Task Force to which, somehow, they had been appointed. "The Task Force was a farce, with poor attendance, and little discussion," said one. Another woman called the Michigan Report "insidious and subversive." . . .

Lest you think that these criticisms emanate from the infamous Little Old Lady in Tennis Shoes, let us turn to the Minnesota Report, of very similar character. A copy of the Minnesota Sex Bias Report was sent for comment to Dr. Rhoda L. Lorand, a clinical psychologist and psychoanalyst in New York City, whose writings are widely published. Dr. Lorand was disgusted.

Were the Minnesota Board of Education to adopt the program drawn up by the Sex Bias Task Force, she declared, the result would be "the promotion of lesbianism, the downgrading of the institution of marriage, of motherhood, childrearing, the nuclear family, the advocacy of single parenthood and communal living, as well as contempt for all occupations and qualities traditionally recognized as feminine." Dr. Lorand proceeded to analyze the Minnesota Report in some detail. . . . [For extracts from Dr. Lorand's analysis, see "Unisex Pressures on Children," below.]

Parents have a right to expect that the schools, in their teaching approaches and selection of instructional materials, will support the values and standards that their children are taught at home [said Commissioner Bell]. And if the schools cannot support those values, they must at least avoid deliberate destruction of them.

For my part, I should like to see some deliberate destruction of Sex Bias Task Forces. State boards of education should reject with cold contempt such pronunciamentos as these "Reports" of Minnesota and Michigan. These baneful follies are the productions of a small handful of female freaks, unrepresentative of American women's convictions generally, but noisy and aggressive.

UNISEX PRESSURES ON CHILDREN [5]

Putting pressure on boys and girls to behave like the opposite sex is placing them under a great strain because these pressures are at odds with biological endowment. Therapists have begun to note the confusion and unhappiness resulting from the blurring of gender-identity. Conflicting pressures between environmental and instinctual

[5] From a letter to the Minnesota Committee for Positive Education. February 3, 1975, by Dr. Rhoda L. Lorand, author, psychologist, Diplomate in Clinical Psychology of the American Board of Professional Psychology. Single copies of critique available from the author, 40 Central Park South, New York, NY 10019. Reprinted by permission.

drives hinders the development of a firm sense of identity as a male or female (an intended goal of Women's Lib) lacking which the individual cannot acquire stability, self-esteem or clear-cut goals. Moreover, it is taking all the joy and excitement out of life. Girls are made to feel ashamed of their longings to be courted and cherished, to be sexually attractive, to look forward to marriage, motherhood and homemaking. Boys are made to feel ashamed of their chivalrous impulses. Feelings of protectiveness towards a girl and of manliness cause them to feel guilty and foolish, resulting in a retreat into passivity while the girls end up unhappily trying to be sexual buddies of the boys. This unisex drive had its beginnings in the hippy movement and has been greatly intensified by all the publicity given by the communications media to the demands and accusations of the feminists (who really should be called masculinists since they despise everything feminine).

These environmental pressures seem to have had a greater effect upon the very young than on anyone else. The latest findings from two large surveys undertaken nationally by the University of Michigan's Institute of Social Research and the equally prestigious National Science Foundation, which measured degrees of satisfaction and dissatisfaction with various aspects of their lives in both men and women, married and single, found that women are just as satisfied with their lives as are men. "Despite the conviction. . . . that women *ought* to feel more frustrated and unrewarded than men, the bulk of the evidence from these studies is that they do not." Also "there is little support in the study results for the belief that housework casts a pall over the life of the housewife or that the working wife suffers from the extraordinary pressures of her two roles." And both studies found that people's greatest satisfactions derive from "those parts of their lives that are the most intimate and personal," in other words, their relationships with spouse and children, whereas the feminists contend that executive power and high earning provide the greatest gratifications and the feeling of being a whole person, for the woman. (*Newsletter* of the Institute for Social Research, University of Michigan, Ann Arbor. Summer '74, Vol. 2, No. 2. "Measuring the Quality of Life in America: A New Frontier for Social Science.") . . .

It should be obvious that the larger and stronger musculature and greater energy of the male sex requires a significantly greater amount of vigorous exercise than is needed or desired by the average girl. However, that does not rule out providing opportunities for the small percentage of girls who enjoy a very vigorous work-out. And the small percentage of boys who loathe the roughness of contact sports should be able to opt for non-contact sports. As for coeducational gym, many New York educators are privately expressing consternation about this innovation which they dare not openly oppose. A TV program on the subject recently showed nine-year olds in coed gym. Both boys and girls expressed to the TV interviewer their dislike of the coed arrangements and their preference for segregated gym classes. The principal of the school then stated that the children would have to learn to like it because there were no longer boys and girls or men and women, there were only children and adults. It's so good to know that the work of those two bunglers, Mother Nature and/or God the Father has finally been set straight.

Electives in introductory shop work designed especially for girls and home economics geared especially to boys' possible needs can be very helpful. But it makes no sense for them each to try to become expert in the other's natural field of excellence . . . on the premise that each young person upon graduation will live in a solitary fortress in a desert, needing to be entirely self-sufficient because there will be no other human being upon whom he can rely for help, cooperation, skills or services of any kind. Friendship, love, devotion, nurturance, cooperation are concepts notably absent from this literature.

TEST SCORES AND UNEQUAL EDUCATION [6]

Reprinted from *U.S. News & World Report.*

A new federally funded report is providing fresh ammunition for women's-rights advocates who claim girls are getting short shrift from the nation's schools.

The study released October 13 [1975] by the National Assessment of Educational Progress shows that, in over-all learning, girls slowly but steadily lose ground to boys from ages nine to seventeen, as measured by nationwide achievement tests.

In the young-adult bracket, the deficit jumps considerably, with women giving about 10 percent fewer correct answers in the math and science exams. At this level, women even score lower in reading and literature—areas in which girls outperform boys during their school years.

In fields where nine-year-old girls have only a small disadvantage, such as social studies and citizenship, the gap widens steadily through the older years, reaching 3 to 4 percent among young adults.

Girls trail on college-board admission tests, too, scoring 46 points lower than boys on a 600-point scale in the math exam last year. In the test of verbal abilities, the girls lost their traditional advantage four years ago, slipping six points below boys among . . . high-school seniors [in 1974].

Why are girls' scores lagging at a time when sex barriers seem to be falling on every side?

"It's certainly not because they're any less intelligent," says Bernice Sandler, who chairs the United States Office of Education's advisory council on women's programs. And she adds: "If anything, research shows that girls reach mental and physical maturity faster than boys."

[6] Article entitled "Girls Lag on Tests: Unequal Education?" *U.S. News & World Report.* 79:54. O. 20, '75.

Pleasing Teacher?

Girls make better grades than boys, but many educators say that this is because they are raised to be neat and "ladylike," which pleases their teachers. Attributes such as these are not much help on standardized tests, however.

On I.Q. tests, girls usually score slightly lower in one measure of abstract reasoning, called "field independence," which involves picking out a visual pattern hidden in a maze of lines. But this alleged weakness shows up mostly in adolescence, and feminists say that all such handicaps probably result from their basic nemesis—traditional notions of femininity. Ms. Sandler describes the pattern this way:

> Girls often score lower and achieve less in later years because society expects them to. Red-blooded boys are supposed to be rambunctious in the early grades, then settle down and start producing in high school. For girls, the pressures are reversed. It's all right for a girl to be the teacher's pet in third grade, but she can't act too smart when it's time to start looking for a man.

Shirley D. McCune, who heads a sex-bias project funded by the National Education Association, says: "It will be an enormous task to get all the unconscious bias out of schools and society. It means we're all going to have to examine our most basic assumptions about masculine and feminine behavior."

Already, Ms. McCune's organization, backed by the nation's largest teachers union, is putting out posters, pamphlets and legal manuals on how to combat subtle "sexism" in school.

One study of grade-school texts, for instance, found that 69 percent of the people in illustrations were males, and 75 percent of the reading stories were about boys. Even in a series of spelling books, consonants were shown as males while "female vowels are . . . yelled at, kicked out, pushed around, used as puppets and told to shut up."

For women tired of such treatment, the organization offers training to make women more assertive and urges teachers to take it. Ms. McCune says: "About 83 percent of our elementary school teachers are women, but 82 percent of their principals are men. Girls' scores will never be as high as boys' unless schools give them something besides stereotypes to aspire to."

Surpassing 1930

Even before the latest test scores, many educators have seen signs that overt discrimination—automatically steering girls toward home economics instead of physics, or toward nursing instead of medicine—is on the wane. Ms. Sandler observes:

"Women now make up about 45 percent of all college students, which finally surpasses the peacetime record of 1930, when there was a lot of fervor left over from the suffrage movement."

Admission of women to law and medical schools is up 200 to 300 percent in five years, while more boys take home economics and nursing.

One factor: new federal rules that make it illegal to exclude students from most courses or activities—including sports—because of their sex. Ms. McCune terms this so-called Title IX Law "potentially one of the most significant pieces of social legislation ever passed by Congress."

Women's advocates concede that the gap between boys' and girls' achievement may never close completely in traditionally male subjects such as math and science. But Ms. Sandler predicts:

"People are going to be surprised what girls and boys both can do once they get over the notion certain things are 'tomboyish' or 'sissy.' "

CHANGING THE STEREOTYPES [7]

She works at a garment factory to supplement her husband's income. She takes care of a home and three children. She has almost enough money to keep chasing the American Dream. Her marriage needs help occasionally, and her children are less than perfect. All in all, at age twenty-eight, she is very nearly the typical modern woman. Statistically, she is a prime candidate for suicide. At the very least, she is in danger of suffering a serious depressive disorder. She feels trapped, powerless and helpless. She is, according to Marcia Guttentag of Harvard University, a victim of sexism.

In most age groups, female admissions to mental hospitals exceed those of males. At community mental health centers, private mental hospitals and general hospitals, depressive disorders are the leading diagnosis for women. Figures from a National Institute of Mental Health survey show that twice as many women as men are diagnosed as suffering from depression. The highest rates of depression occur among women between the ages of twenty-one and thirty-five.

Depression can lead to suicide, and throughout the developed world suicide attempters are overwhelmingly young females between the ages of twenty and thirty. Reviewing data on depression and suicide, Guttentag concludes that "it is the young, married, working blue-collar mother who is most likely to be depressed." And the risk of depression for these women has increased dramatically during the past two decades.

Women's entry into the labor market has also increased markedly during the past twenty years, and that may be part of the problem. Sexist attitudes have long kept women

[7] Article entitled "Sexism Is Depressing," by Robert J. Trotter, free-lance writer. *Science News.* 108:173-4. S. 13, '75. Reprinted with permission from *Science News,* the weekly news magazine of science, copyright 1975 by Science Service, Inc.

from achieving educational and occupational equality. When they do work, women are often placed in underpaid, unsatisfying positions while still being expected to fulfill the traditional sexist family roles. As a result, a woman might easily begin to feel trapped, powerless, stressed and depressed.

If these mental health findings are viewed in relation to sex-role stereotypes [says Guttentag], the conclusion is inescapable that it is sex-stereotyped familial and socio-emotional roles which, in addition to the occupational burdens that women now carry, are causing the greatly intensified stresses they experience.

For many years now, feminists have argued that sexual stereotyping is psychologically damaging. Guttentag has attempted to prove this point with mounds of mental health data. But even if the point is proved, can anything be done to change the situation? Laws and regulations, such as the still unratified Equal Rights Amendment, have helped to curb overt institutional discrimination, but sexism continues to exist as an informal part of cultural and family practices. Guttentag contends this type of sexism has to be prevented if mental health damage is to be averted.

Even young adolescents, both boys and girls, show the damaging effects sex stereotypes can have on their self-concepts and on the life possibilities that they believe are open to them. It thus seems that prevention of sexism should begin at an early age, and one logical place to start would be in the schools.

If schools do provide the best setting for the prevention of sexism, how can they best be used in such prevention? Does the age of the child make a difference? Who should be the targets of preventive efforts—should they be equally directed toward boys and girls? Guttentag and her colleagues have designed and implemented an experimental program that answers these questions. Results of the study . . . [appear in *Undoing Sex Stereotypes: Research & Re-*

sources for Education. McGraw-Hill. 1976]. Highlights of
the findings were presented at the recent conference on the
prevention of psychopathology [the Vermont Conference
on the Primary Prevention of Psychopathology, 1975].

Three school systems in the Boston area were selected
for the six-week study. They represented different social
and ethnic backgrounds. Three age groups were selected:
five-, nine- and fourteen-year-olds (kindergarten, fifth and
ninth grades). They represented different stages of cognitive development. The aim of the study was to see whether
it was possible, through the use of curricula, teachers and
peer groups, to modify children's sex role stereotypes in
three areas: occupational, familial and socio-emotional.

The children's sexual stereotypes were measured in a
number of ways: Projective questions were used, such as:
"Tell me about a typical day when you are thirty years old."
"Describe a day in the life of a typical woman; a typical
man." The answers were used to determine the children's
understanding of adult roles and the extent to which they
felt they would conform to such roles. The children were
asked to tell about the jobs they thought men and women
could have and to describe what men and women like per-
sonally (socio-emotional qualities). They were asked to tell
stories using the characteristics of the opposite sex and to
tell researchers what they thought real girls and boys were
like, what ideal girls and boys were like and what they
themselves were like. Children in experimental and control groups were questioned before and after the intervention program.

The intervention consisted of specially devised curricula
that were integrated into regular English and social studies
work and into the entire day of the kindergarteners. Books,
plays, records and special projects were included. Teachers
received training in how to work with children in nonsexist
patterns, such as maintaining a high rate of interaction with
both girls and boys. Observers recorded teacher-pupil inter-
actions before, during and after the intervention. Teachers

were also rated on their enthusiasm and use of curriculum material.

The social class and ethnic backgrounds of the children made no difference in their initial sex-role stereotypes. Having a working mother, even a high-status working mother, made no differnce. Even the kindergarten children, regardless of their backgrounds, had highly stereotyped views. This, says Guttentag, suggests that even at young ages children have learned cultural stereotypes, probably through television and their peers, and that these are more powerful than the influence of the family.

The intervention effort worked differently on the three groups. Initially, the kindergarteners were quite stereotyped about occupational roles. They emphasized that men and women had different jobs and spent their time doing different things. A woman could not be a mother and an aviator. Fathers always went to work, except on weekends when they played with the children. Following the intervention, the kindergarteners had increased significantly in their ability to understand that the same job could be held by either a man or a woman. The girls, especially, were more likely to place men in interpersonal jobs such as social worker, teacher or sales clerk. The children did not, however, change their attitudes toward the family and emotional roles that men and women play.

Fifth graders were the least stereotyped of the three groups. They believed that women could have jobs, but that they might not succeed at them. They nearly always put men and women into sex stereotyped private routines and hobbies. Boys and men were ascribed particularly restrictive socio-emotional roles. They never admitted to having any problems and saw themselves as active in sports and economically successful. Girls readily accepted an emotional emphasis as an important part of their role. They also showed a slight tendency toward negative self esteem—they felt they were not as beautiful as they should be.

In the fifth grade, the intervention was most effective

with girls. Their belief that women could have varied and
successful careers was strengthened. There were also changes
in their attitudes towards men's roles. The boys, however,
were very little changed.

Ninth graders were the most stereotyped of all. They believed that interpersonal and emotional qualities were essential for women. Although the girls supported women in
occupations, the boys were suspicious of employed women.
Girls more often presented the women in a dual marriage
and career situation. Ninth graders tended to react negatively to the intervention. Most boys' views became more
stereotyped after the intervention. And peer-group support
for the boys was particularly strong in upholding the sexist
attitudes. From these results, says Guttentag, it appears that
a little intervention of a nonsexist type may be worse than
none at all for ninth-grade boys.

Perhaps the most meaningful and relevant finding of
the study, says Guttentag, came from examination of
changes in individual classrooms. The amount of attitude
change was closely correlated to the individual teacher's
effectiveness in implementing the curriculum. In other
words, the teacher who cared about the issue of sexism in
roles and society and who used the curriculum regularly
and creatively, was able to change the attitudes of students
even in a brief six-week intervention period.

Although the girls at all ages were the most responsive
to the program, it was the boys' sex-role stereotypes that
were most in need of change. But as is the case in most types
of intervention, those who need it most were the least likely
to change. Even so, in classrooms where there were active
and committed teachers, there were changes in all children,
even the boys, and change occurred even at the most resis-
tant age.

It is clear [concludes Guttentag] that the schools can be used
in a primary preventive role. Even a brief nonsexist intervention,
implemented schoolwide, can have marked effects on sexist stereotypes of children and adolescents.

It looks very much as though for the young, married, working mother, we are confronted with a time-lag problem. The occupational roles of women have changed more quickly than have their family-role definitions. This is particularly true for blue-collar women. Given the rapidly changing labor market participation rates for women, less sexist definitions of male and female family and socio-emotional roles could have an ameliorative effect on the stresses which many women now experience. . . . The schools are one socializing instrument which can immediately serve in the primary prevention of sexism.

III. YOUNG ADULTHOOD

EDITOR'S INTRODUCTION

The articles in this section are concerned with the period of self-awareness in terms of society and of choices to be made. Young adulthood is the time when many crucial life decisions are made, adult personal identity is being established, and the first serious female-male relationships are being developed—the most crucial time in an individual's life development.

The first article, by the social critic Vance Packard, published in 1968, reflects the discomfort felt by young men of high school and college age in the face of the most recent upsurge of the women's movement. In this time of questioning of many values, it is doubly difficult for young men to have their traditional roles and expectations upset.

The second selection, from Caroline Bird's *Born Female,* was also written during the late sixties. The excerpt discusses changes wrought by the new femininsm in the lives of men and women, the overall effect on the culture of our time, and the nature of the culture that seems to be evolving—a variety of domestic patterns including, for many families in which wife and husband are equally interested in work and professional development, the androgynous lifestyle deplored by traditionalists.

A related issue—the right of women to retain their original names (and individual identities) if they choose to do so—is the topic of the next article, by Judy Klemesrud. The final selection, by Jean Stapleton and Richard Bright, offers practical advice, in the context of the late 1970s, to young people who seek equality in marriage.

THE YOUNG MALE REACTS [1]

While the spotlight recently has been on the "New Female," the young male in transition has been facing gnawing problems. He not only has to cope with those new females, but also must cope with other upsetting new elements in his way of life.

It is easy for the young male to perceive that masculinity counts for less in the home, at work, and even in bed. Some years ago when eighteen family experts were invited to list the most important changes affecting the modern family, they listed in second place (after divorce) the "decline in authority of husbands and fathers." The decline is continuing. In 1968 sociologist Jessie Bernard observed, "There is beginning to be recognition of the fact that the change in the status of women may have a deleterious effect on men."

Some males feel the new pressures much more than others. But as a generalization, a distinction made by psychologist Theodor Reik seems fair. He said that in our civilization women are afraid that they will be considered only women—and men are afraid they will not be considered men enough.

Vis-à-vis the new females, young males are being invited to move over. They have the option of adjusting philosophically to their new role expectations . . . or pretending that nothing is happening . . . or fighting back. Meanwhile they must maintain their aplomb under scrutiny. Family sociologist David Mace suggests—as one symptom of the new condition—that the point of suspense in the modern novel is no longer focused on whether she will or she won't, but on whether he can or he can't.

Many young males not only feel their adequacy threatened, but are confused as to what really the modern world

[1] Excerpts from *The Sexual Wilderness*, by Vance Packard, author, editor, journalist. McKay. '68. p 118-26, 133-4. Copyright © 1968 by Vance Packard. Reprinted by permission of the publisher.

expects of them. Officially they are still expected to be strong, bold, gallant to women, masterful breadwinners, and protectors of weaker women and children. The ideal male is primarily a product of civilization. Primitive societies tend not to make so much of sex differences.

In some Western societies we still have laws on the books that affirm the male to be the lord and master. In Italy the female can legally be disciplined by father, brother, or husband; and she is required to live where her husband decides to live. The Italian wife who tries to kill an unfaithful husband will be treated as an ordinary criminal in court; while the husband who murders an unfaithful wife will be viewed as having committed a crime of honor and be punished lightly, if at all. Much the same double standard in dealing with husband-wife assaults prevails in the courts of Texas, USA.

There is evidence that males never have been as dominant and superior-minded in coping with females as they often like to pretend. Early psychiatrists made much of the "penis envy" of women. More recently, several have been impressed by the "vagina envy" of males. Keith Fischer, psychoanalyst of Philadelphia, advises: "There is magic in the vagina and the woman's capacity to have a baby. Some men get sick when their wives get pregnant. And the man usually calls the newborn 'my baby.' " Other psychiatrists have shown a new interest in the primitive ritual called the couvade, which was reported decades ago by anthropologists working with primitive tribes. A nineteenth century report on the ritual as practiced among Indians of Guiana and reported by Sir E. F. Im Thurn described the ritual as follows:

The woman works as usual up until a few hours before birth; she goes to the forest with some women and there the birth takes place. In a few hours she is up and at work. . . . As soon as the child is born the father takes to his hammock and abstains from work, from meat and from all food but weak gruel of cassava meal, from smoking, from washing himself, and above all from touching weapons of any sort, and is nursed and cared for by all the women of the place. . . . This goes on for days, sometimes weeks.

Professor of psychiatry Bruno Bettelheim in discussing such rituals suggests that women, being emotionally satisfied by actually demonstrating their ability to create new life, can be indulgent with male make-believe. Men, he said, need the make-believe to fill the emotional vacuum created by their inability to bear children. Sociologist Gunnar Boalt of the University of Stockholm suggests that women's main biological drive is to have children, not to have husbands.

In any case, young males today are seeing that many of the historic male prerogatives are now dubious. A number of psychotherapists have noted that there seems to be an increase in the number of passive, dependent males among their patients. That would not, of course, necessarily apply to the general male population. But historian Charles W. Ferguson in tracing the male's traditional sources of confidence and power states:

> Virtually all the conditions that produced and fostered masculine philosophy and sentiment have vanished. As far as their day-to-day existence is concerned, most men have moved from a physical and violent world into a sensitive and delicate one. Energy has been transferred from muscles to molecules. The new atom has replaced the old Adam.

The changed world of the male arising from the liberating of women can be seen vividly in Japan, where for centuries the male has been monarch of the home. When I was in Japan a few years ago, a group of business executives were invited to discuss what aspect of the traditional way of life the Japanese most stubbornly wanted to preserve. One man blurted out, "We don't want to change our women!" Younger men in the group told me later that they, the younger ones, no longer insist that their wives follow them if they walk in public. In fact, they take their wives out to dinner about once a month and walk with them side

by side. They added that they are sometimes kidded by
older people the next day about being seen with their
mistresses.

The new assertiveness of females arising from near-
equality and such liberating influences as conception-control
has probably most startled young males in the area of physical intimacy (for those who have explored that area). We
might suppose that males should be delighted by evidence
that millions of young unmarried females of good backgrounds are becoming more sexually playful and less inhibited. And many do count this as a very great gain. Very few
societies in recorded history have witnessed such a phenomenon as a widespread pattern. Many young males, once they
have reflected on the matter and contemplate the future,
are not sure they should be enchanted. They hear from psychiatrists, if they haven't learned for themselves, that the
sexually demanding woman can be a formidable one. . . .

Young males see abundant evidence almost every night
on television that the traditional image of the masterful
male has been scuttled by the producers of family-comedy
shows. A few facts of life about television may account for
this: (1) there are more female than male viewers; (2) in
homes where husband and wife are watching, the wife usually controls the selection of programs; (3) wives are about
five times as likely as husbands to be potential purchasers
of the products being advertised.

Mass communications specialist Robert C. O'Hara, of
the University of South Florida, finds that in the typical
family comedy the male is incapable of handling even the
simplest tasks without making a mess of things. When, as
often happens, he does something against the judgment of
his wife, disaster invariably ensues, and she has to straighten
things out. In "Bewitched" it is the miracle-performing wife
who keeps saving her husband from disgracing himself. One
investigator after a study of TV comedy formulas found
that an all-pervading one was "The Jackass Formula."
Under this barrel-of-laffs formula, the men cook up a

scheme . . . the wives perceive it can't work . . . the men go ahead anyway . . . it doesn't work . . . the wives save the situation.

In 1967 TV commercials depicted a series of baseball celebrities such as Yogi Berra beaming as they used their wives' hair spray. On one network commercial, the husband was asked why he bought Borax. He explained, "My wife told me to buy it and so I bought it." And there was the bald husband looking solemn as his radiant wife explained to viewers, "This is my husband Jim. He may not look like much to you. But I love him." And then she demonstrated why, by feeding him some Temp Tee whipped cream cheese; the bald, solemn husband went wild, kissing the lovely hand that was feeding him.

All this, of course, is surface froth. There are, however, fundamental reasons for many males to be unsettled about the roles emerging for them in modern life. One is the shrinkage of ways to validate themselves in ways that have reassured them in the past. A girl wants to be called a girl as long as plausible, a boy wants to be called a man as soon as plausible. . . .

The frontier and the sea have largely disappeared as places where restless young males could find self-realization. And it is becoming increasingly unsafe for society to let young males have access to those traditional emblems of masculinity, guns. One of the saddest lines in contemporary drama was in Arthur Miller's movie *The Misfits*. The character played by Clark Gable had made his living capturing wild horses, but they were now hard to find, and the best market for those captured was the dog-food industry. He muttered, "I've got to find another way to be alive—if there is one anywhere." In our new society the cow puncher is being replaced by the key puncher as the figure close to the center of free enterprise.

In the TV commercial the male still, after lighting up, heads his horse off into the rugged challenges of Marlboro Country. But how rugged is the West?

Sociologist Reuel Denney comments that no young males enjoy the imagery of the rugged individual more than those in the arid rural states. But he added that most of these states would hardly break even if it were not for federal subsidies for farm products; metal and water resources; income from tourist bars, dude ranches, and gambling; and graft on the public lands.

There are still rugged or adventuresome jobs—as in ranching, truck-driving, carpentry, sponge-diving, piloting planes, etc.—but a more typical enterprising young male of the late 1960s is shown in the TV commercial for Sun-Up shaving lotion. He gives a Tarzan cry, leaps over the living-room balcony, and starts to work carrying his briefcase. The son of such a commuter probably has only a vague idea how Father validates himself. This raises interesting questions about what kind of men such sons will be when they grow up.

If perchance he rises toward the top of a major business enterprise, it doesn't bring much glory, because executives of large corporations increasingly are trained to be semi-anonymous, bland, soft-spoken, non-oddball team players.

Or, if he succeeds in a job requiring technical skills, he confronts the uneasy fact that with the blinding speed of technological innovation his skills will probably be largely obsolete in a decade or so and he may have to learn new skills.

The young man's image of himself as a future community leader is likely to be weakly fixed. He has observed that husbands in his neighborhood who commute to work leave much of the family's representation in the community to the wife, if there is any representation.

If he is thoughtful, the young male may also perceive that many of the traits most necessary to our society's healthy functioning today are traits long considered to be female rather than male. Margaret Mead mentions these three virtues, long regarded as more appropriate for women, as being necessary today: patience, endurance, steadfastness.

Along this same line, Richard Farson, director of the Western Behavioral Sciences Institute, suggests that women are better suited for the world of the 1980s because they are less encumbered by the Protestant ethic, under which worth is only possible by hard, painstaking work. With the electronics revolution he anticipates that less and less time or energy will be needed for hard work. There will be more emphasis upon finding fulfillment through human relationships and the enjoyment of culture—both of which, he contends, come more naturally to women.

We should note, too, the quite new conditions under which modern young males are reared. In earlier societies in the USA—where father was dominant and male relatives were near—the boy was mainly under male influences in his formative years. This is still true in many working-class homes. But in the homes of the mobile, corporate, white-collar toiler, management of girls and boys is left mainly to the mother. Disciplining is more likely to come from mother than father, and so is more likely to take the form of a withdrawal of love than of a thrashing.

In his first years in school the young male is still in an overwhelmingly female-dominated environment, and in co-educational schools he must compete with same-age girls who have matured more rapidly than he has. His schooling—and thus usually his dependency upon parents—will extend well past the time he achieves physical maturity. As family specialist Lester Kirkendall points out, "The chances of the modern lad of eighteen gaining community recognition for his masculine achievements through economic and vocational activities are severely limited."

In counting major changes in the maturing male's world we should note, too, the substantial erosion of uniquely male habitats. Australia is one of the few modern countries left where men dominate everyday life, assign women to clearly supporting roles, and congregate regularly in their sex-segregated male haunts, including pubs and clubs.

In the USA, clubs and restaurants still reserved exclusively for males are becoming exceedingly scarce. Women are following men into saloons; and the saloons soon become lounges. If the husband goes fishing or hunting, the wife increasingly is likely to go along and even want to fish or hunt herself.

One of the most respected of all sanctuaries for young American males, the poolroom, declined for decades and—typical of the times—its recent resurgence has involved a desexualization of the institution. It is now more likely to be called a "billiard lounge" with wall-to-wall carpeting and sexually ambiguous decor. Sociologist Ned Polsky, however, doubts the sport can thrive for long on a bisexual basis, because women simply see it as a passing fad, while to the bachelor male it has deep emotional meaning as a refuge from women.

Perhaps the most startling desexualization of a sport can be seen in the journals devoted to wrestling. The magazine *Wrestling Illustrated* now carries on its front cover in small type under the title these words, "Combined with *Girl Wrestling*." One recent front cover carried the pictures of 5 wrestlers. Four were male, and the other was a female, Brenda Scott. She authored an article of lament entitled "Men Are Afraid to Date Me." In the article she drew upon her psychological insights to conclude that her problem stemmed from the fact that males like to think they are the stronge ones. . . .

Meanwhile, some of the more sophisticated male magazines provided their readers with material that exhibited glowering hostility or amiable paternalism toward females. A good deal of their content seemed designed to denigrate females. The mood was often competitive or defensive and seemed to suggest a drive by the males to protect their long-dominant position.

Playboy usually presents women as playthings, pleasant to pet. On the other hand, *True* quite regularly has been depicting women either as the adversaries of man or as a breed whose come-uppance is overdue. Each month it has a regular feature, It's a Man's World, dedicated to keeping males informed and to keeping "the little woman firmly in her place."

On the front cover of its February 1967 issue *True* asked its readers if their wives were spying on them. One of its major efforts at keeping the little woman firmly in her place was an article in its February 1965 issue entitled: "The Female Fears That Bind a Man." It was illustrated by a cartoon of a sweating man in harness trying to move forward while hauling a nest containing his brood, with his wife looking fearfully backward. The thesis was summed up at the outset: "Women are afraid of all kinds of things. Financial insecurity is only one of them. Women are afraid of physical hardship, physical danger, illness, the dark, lizards and mice and insects to list a few." The author, Max Gunther, acknowledged that this was the way women were constituted and there wasn't much a man could do about it. But he added, "When female fears prevent a man from doing things he wants to do, it's time to blow the whistle, time for a declaration of male independence from womanish worries!"

In contrast, the leading US women's magazines during the 1960s devoted very little space to trying to put the male in his place. Instead, when discussing male-female relationships they seemed to be trying thoughtfully to understand what was going on.

Considering their surgent position, they could afford to be magnanimous.

NEW CHOICES, NEW ROLES [2]

We were trying to explain to a friend why some employers think it is right to pay men more than women. "It's because men have to support women," we reminded her.

[2] Excerpts from *Born Female: The High Cost of Keeping Women Down*, by Caroline Bird, free-lance writer and member of a public relations firm. McKay. '68. p 167-73, 183-8. Copyright © 1968, 1970, 1973 by Caroline Bird. Reprinted by permission of the publisher.

She looked so puzzled that we jokingly repeated the Old Masculinist answer to pleas for equal pay: "After all, *you* don't have to support your husband, but *he* has to support you."

"Does he?" she said with transparent innocence. And it turned out that she really did not know the laws of family support.

"You just ask your husband," we told her. "It's really so. He has to support you. By law."

For several weeks afterward we told the story to working wives as a believe-it-or-not anecdote. But many of them found nothing peculiar about her question. A surprising percentage just had never thought about marriage in terms of legal support.

"What about alimony?" we asked one newly married girl. "Why do divorced wives get alimony?"

"Do they still?" she asked, with enormous indifference. "I thought that had been abolished."

Her comment reflected the increasing opposition to alimony. The proverbial golddigger who takes a divorced husband for all he is worth is giving way to the woman who would rather support herself than accept money from a man she does not love. As one talented divorcee put it, "Who cares about money? You can make that." Young college-educated couples do not expect a wife to press her legal right to alimony unless there is some reason why she cannot support herself.

The old common-law notion that divorced wives deserve alimony as a sex right was giving way to the concept of reciprocal support based on need and ability to pay regardless of sex or fault. In 1970, at least 18 states, including California, permitted alimony to men under certain circumstances. Some local welfare laws make an employed wife responsible for the support of a husband who would otherwise become a public charge. And support works both ways, theoretically at least, in some European countries.

One of the young brides we queried thought the family-support laws we told her about were reciprocal in this country, too. "If my husband supports me," she reasoned with us, "don't I have to support him, too?"

For these young women, at least, the sex-for-support bargain is a thing of the past. They have not married for money. Their husbands have not married for sex. These young couples do not think they have a vocational relationship. They think of themselves, rather, as companions, carrying the androgynous pattern of school life into marriage, family, and work. They marry almost as early as the girls who expect to make marriage a career, and like them they get a job or go on studying. But they work or study for different reasons.

Instead of waiting on table to put a husband through medical school, these young, college-educated brides seek out jobs which pay in experience and opportunity rather than in cash. They work for token pay or no pay at all on small-town newspapers, in nonprofit organizations, in the Peace Corps or poverty programs. They make jobs for themselves in museums or in local government or community colleges. Like alert young men beginning careers, they are working for the work itself, for what it can teach them, or where it can lead.

Because her work is important, this kind of young woman often marries a man in her own field, often a fellow student or fellow worker. Graduate students marry each other. Law students marry law students. Medical students marry medical students. College faculty members marry each other. Research workers marry each other. Actors and actresses marry each other. In 1966, one of the engineers inspecting telephone installations in Orange County, California, was a woman married to another telephone company employee. These wives are not helpmeets of their husbands. If they happen to have the same employer, they are colleagues, even competitors.

The first home these couples live in is temporary, and they readily accept barracks-like public housing for its convenience, or even a furnished room for the duration of the course, the project, or their first, trial jobs. Housework is minimized and shared.

They often head for the big city where both can find work. One may go to school while the other earns, but the earner is not always the wife, and the arrangement is short-term.

If they are in the same profession, they are tempted to work together, like the famous French scientists Marie and Pierre Curie, who discovered radium, and the English social reformers, Sidney and Beatrice Webb. Some contemporary couples have become famous, among them the theater team Lynne Fontanne and Alfred Lunt, Oregon Senators Richard L. and Maurine Neuberger, historians Will and Ariel Durant, Lila and DeWitt Wallace, founders of the *Reader's Digest,* and Robert and Helen Lynd, the sociologists who immortalized Muncie, Indiana, in *Middletown.* Thousands of less celebrated couples have demonstrated that two can combine marriage and a career more successfully than either might have done working alone. Many pediatricians are husband-and-wife teams who can spell each other on phone calls and office hours so that they both have time to spend with their own children. Anthropologists who marry each other make a handy team for field work which needs investigators of both sexes.

Usually, however, it is impractical for the couple to work together, and as both careers develop, it may be hard for them to stay in the same part of the country. But it can be done. In 1967 Bob and Barbara Williams were serving as Army nurses within enemy mortar range in Vietnam and living together in a hut made out of materials Bob had scrounged. They met and married while studying nursing at the Columbus State Hospital in Ohio. When Bob was drafted three months after their marriage, Barbara volunteered and joined him overseas a few months later. Both were First Lieutenant Army surgical nurses.

Sometimes it is the husband who moves. Men teachers have found jobs in Los Angeles or New York to be with actress wives. Henry Luce accompanied Clare Boothe Luce when she was Ambassador to Italy and spent most of her term with her, managing Time, Inc., from an office in Rome. In 1966, Ambassador-at-Large Ellsworth Bunker took up official residence with his bride, Carol Laise, the US Ambassador to Nepal, Asia, because residence was a requirement of her job but not of his.

For the affluent, air travel can solve the geographical problem, at least temporarily. When Rosemary Park, president of Barnard College in New York, married Dr. Milton V. Anastos, professor of Byzantine Greek at the University of California at Los Angeles in 1966, she kept in touch with her new husband by cross-country jet until Barnard found a new president. Then she got a job near her husband's as vice-chancellor for educational planning and programs at UCLA.

Two-career families may have children, but they do not build their whole lives around them. "It's simply not true that they are as involved with their families as women who want to stay at home," Alice Rossi of the Department of Social Relations at Johns Hopkins University reports after studying 15,000 women three years out of college who planned careers. She found that the career-committed women didn't want as many children, on the average, as the homemakers, and that they were far more willing to let others care for their children.

In two-career homes, the babies do not come all at once, at the beginning of the marriage, but in phase with the wife's work commitments. Teachers can plan to have their babies during vacations; Professor Ilse Lipschutz of Vassar has had four children without losing time from class. Almost every graduating class now has pregnant wives in the procession, and sometimes a husband and wife are graduated together while their small child looks on. In June 1967, for instance, Stephanie Beech and her husband Charles were graduated from Park College, in Parkville, Missouri, five months after their baby was born. Stephanie was able to make up the month of classes she missed and to do her part earning the money needed to keep them both in school. She and her husband shared her job on the early-morning shift at a cafeteria. He did it while she was in the hospital, and after the baby was born, they took turns, one doing the job, the other the baby's three o'clock feeding.

Many employers believe that pay isn't an inducement to a woman worker because "you can't compete with a baby." The fact is, of course, that you can. With money. The more money a woman makes, the more likely she is to come back to work after a baby. "You can afford to stay home with your baby," a woman executive once told her secretary. "At my salary, I can't." The better-paid a woman, the more apt she is to keep working.

Fathers in two-career homes are often closer to their children than men whose wives make a career out of motherhood. They share child care in various ways. A woman television director in New York who is married to an optometrist spends her days off with their two boys while he keeps his office open. On the days she has to work, he closes his office and takes care of the boys. In 1966 he took them over alone while she tested a job in California. In another family, the mother is a public relations executive and the father is a teacher. Like mothers who teach, he uses his shorter day and longer vacations to spend more time with the children. Husbands with flexible schedules cook, run errands, babysit, and shop for wives who have less control over their time.

Two-career families either forgo the social life wives usually arrange or share the work of organizing it.

Two-career homes undoubtedly form the character of children in a different way than homes where mothers do most of the rearing alone. Mother-child relationships are cooler than the early Freudians advocated, and parents have more rights than they have recently enjoyed in America, particularly rights to privacy and a shared adult life. Dr. Rossi speculates that wives in two-career families are more interested in a relationship with their husband than the homemaking women, who tend to seek their major satisfaction from their children.

Sociologists report that they can't find any important difference between the children of mothers who work and the children of mothers who stay at home. In fact, in some cases they discovered that the children suffered in homes where the mothers wanted to work, but stayed at home out of a mistaken sense of duty. They also found that the children of working mothers were sometimes more self-reliant than children reared by full-time, child-centered mothers.

Two-career couples are New Feminists, but they are not militant. The women are more friendly to men than the pioneer career women, partly because they have undisputed control over the timing of their children and no longer need to fear the strength and spontaneity of their own sex drives. They are not missionary about their lifestyle, and tend to minimize and even ignore their departure from the traditional pattern. . . .

"There is nothing inherently feminine about mixing a given batch of materials, exposing it to a definite temperature for a definite time, and producing a cake," Dr. Rebecca Sparling, of General Dynamics, declared. "There is nothing inherently masculine in mixing a batch of materials, exposing it to a definite temperature for a given time, and producing *iron castings*. I have done both and find them satisfying occupations."

Opportunities for women in occupations once reserved for men were publicized by banks, government, and companies that were having a hard time finding qualified employees. Newspapers cooperated by giving publicity to any "first" for a woman that her organization's public information officer could verify. In the summer of 1967, we clipped, at random, news of the "first" woman assistant vice president of the New York Federal Reserve Bank, "one of the first" woman court psychologists in New York State, the "first" woman pilot to be hired by a French government airline, and the "only" woman to be elected to the board of governors of the American Oil Society. Women jockeys began to ride at American tracks in 1969 and one competed in the 1970 Kentucky Derby. By then the "firsts" had become more common and newspapers were less likely to dwell on the anomaly of a woman in the role.

The . . . trend toward androgyny is a general *desegregation of the sexes.* Stag sanctuaries are being challenged, most often by their own members. Luncheon clubs in most cities are quietly beginning to admit women or are making it easier for them to use their facilities. In 1967, the National Press Club invited women to its traditionally stag "Congressional Night" honoring members of Congress. Previously, even women members of Congress had been excluded. . . .

Professional and special-purpose organizations formed by women when the barriers against them were high are rethinking their reasons for existing. Members of the National Association of Bank Women, Theta Sigma Phi, the women's journalistic fraternity, and American Women in Radio and Television began to wonder if they should not try to join the men's organizations. Many distinguished women simply did not bother with *Who's Who of American Women.* If they weren't well-known enough to be in *Who's Who in America,* they didn't want to be in a woman's Who's Who.

The Medical Women's Association addressed itself to public issues on which it felt women doctors could make a special contribution, such as sex education and medical

The league . . . was named after the woman who, in 1855, became the first woman in the United States known to retain her maiden name. Her friend, Olympia Brown, a minister after whom the Wisconsin group was named, is believed to be the second American woman to keep her birth name after she married.

Why the big interest in maiden names right now? "Because women are occupying more important jobs than they used to," replied Miss Lyle, a retired actress and writer who has used her maiden name since the 1920s. "This whole new interest in the status of women has aroused women's interest in their own individual being."

This new trend is showing up in newspapers' society [col]umns, as more and more brides are declaring in their [we]dding announcements their intention to use their maiden [nam]es after marriage.

[A]mong those whose announcements recently included [this] information was Mary Ann (Mazie) Livingston Dela-[no] Cox, whose brother, Edward, is married to Tricia [...] Miss Cox, who teaches architectural design at Smith [...], was married last September to Brinkley Stimson [...] an architect.

"Contributing to Partnership"

[A]delia Moore, daughter of the Right Rev. Paul [...] Episcopal Bishop of New York, who married [...]y in October 1972; and Pamela Howard, daugh-[ter of the p]resident of the Scripps-Howard newspaper and [...] chain, who was married last November [1973] [to ...]. Potter, a book publisher.

[... contr]ibuting to a partnership, and partners don't [... each oth]er's names," said Miss Howard, a freelance [...], my husband has been married before, and [... ma]ny people in the world who have lots of ex-[... I jus]t didn't see any reason to take his name

---

education for women. Women were, of course, admitted to the American Medical Association, which represents the profession as a whole, without question, but they were underrepresented in its House of Delegates and on its committees. In June 1967, the Episcopal Church Women of Iowa disbanded because they felt it would be "more efficient" to work with the men of the church. In September 1967, the National Secretaries Association, a formerly all-female organization, broke with "one of its basic precepts" and admitted C. J. "Bucky" Helmer Jr., a man who had been trying to get in for years. When he was rejected in 1964, he had formed the Male Secretaries of America and built it up to 315 members.

Other customs which separate the sexes are also being challenged. The most dramatic example can be seen in the liberal wing of the Roman Catholic Church. Nuns are no longer invariably hidden away from the world, as traditional wives used to be. Some are doffing their habits. . . .

During the 1960s, the notion of cloister has been breaking down so fast on college campuses that graduates of the 1950s can hardly recognize their own alma maters today. Rules restricting the hours and activities of women in college dormitories are being relaxed and even abolished. Girls are rebelling against the whole idea of living under supervision, and on many campuses have taken apartments together "off campus," and, on some avant-garde campuses, even with men students. College authorities have tried to avoid the issue with parents or the press, but many have given up any attempt to regulate the private lives of their students. . . .

The United Nations Educational, Scientific, and Cultural Organization reported a worldwide trend toward coeducation. The whole trend [toward ending all-female and all-male schools and colleges in the United States] is encouraged by the rising proportion of college faculty that has been educated in coeducational colleges as well as by the number of students who come from coeducational high schools rather than sexually divided prep schools.

Segregated recreation is dying out along with segregated

education. Most men no longer stop at bars to drink together after work; instead, they hurry home to help with the children, have a drink with their wives, or watch television. Poolrooms, once refuges for men, have had to try to attract family groups in order to stay in business. Girls are going on camping and biking trips with men friends, as they long have done in Europe.

The de-emphasis on sex is also altering supposedly immutable feminine biology. Now that her sex no longer determines a woman's social destiny, now that she chooses whether to conceive or even bear a child already conceived, she has fewer miscarriages, menstrual pains, and "female" troubles, real or imaginary, than when her status depended on her sexual relationship to a man. In their places, however, doctors are noticing a rise in the proportion of women afflicted with ulcers, asthma, respiratory diseases, and alcoholism—health problems formerly considered male. . . .

These trends to the androgynous life—longer years for women without childbirth, more education for women, more work outside the home, less segregation of the sexes—are all part of a more general trend to individual choice. We are affluent enough and command sufficient technological knowledge to be able to live in many different ways. There will be more styles of life, and more people will be able to enjoy the style that fits them best. The choice is especially rich for women, if only because their old role is breaking down and no single new role is taking its place.

A MATTER OF IDENTITY [3]

When Jane Burrell got married last June [1973], she decided to continue using her maiden name. The ground didn't shake, her in-laws didn't disown her, her marriage didn't dissolve. In fact, her husband, Michael Brunson, a

[3] Article by Judy Klemesrud, feature writer. New York *Times*. p 48. Ap. 10, '74. Copyright by The New York Times Company. Reprinted by permission.

sales trainee for a printing company, was very much in fa of her decision.

"I just decided that my name before was very imp to me, and that I didn't want to assume someone els tity," said Miss Burrell, of Brooklyn, a twenty-thre portfolio assistant at a Manhattan investment ba pany. "I wanted to retain my identity; I thi loses something of herself if she doesn't."

Time was when the woman who contin maiden name after marriage was considere iconoclastic, and perhaps a bit of a w course, unless she was an actress or a w kind of professional.

Nowadays, in the wake of the wo ment, more and more rank-and-fi Jane Burrell are continuing to born with. Others are returnin while still others are using their dle names (as in Jane Doe maiden and their married n

This game of the name cent causes célèbres of the nist lawyers busy and organizations to help These include Cente rington, Illinois; chusetts; and the Wisconsin.

"Unques maiden-na enty-five organiz establi nam about i

Only one state, Hawaii, has a statute expressly requiring that a woman take her husband's name after marriage. In other states, any woman may continue to use her maiden name after marriage. No court action is necessary, for under English common law (and New York State's Civil Rights Law) any person may use any name desired as long as it is not done for the purpose of fraud or unfair competition.

"The custom of a woman taking her husband's name upon marriage is so widespread that many people believe it is required by law," said Emily Jane Goodman, a lawyer who is volunteer director of the Women's Law Center [New York City].

The most important thing is consistency and continuity in a woman's use of her own name, Miss Goodman stressed; she must be careful never to adopt her husband's name for any purpose. Switching back and forth may give a government agency the right to choose which name it wishes a woman to use on her official documents, she said.

What about the married woman who has used her husband's name for several years, and then decides she wants to use her maiden name? According to a Women's Law Center brochure on name change, such a woman need not get divorced or separated, and she need not go to court. She merely starts using her own name again.

Changing Bank Accounts

In practical terms, this means she should go to her bank and have her accounts changed to her own name. (If the bank refuses, she can withdraw all her money and deposit it in another bank.) Then she should notify all of her friends, relatives and creditors, as well as Social Security, her employer, the Motor Vehicle Bureau, Board of Elections, and all other persons who might be interested.

A recent publication, *Booklet for Women Who Wish to Determine Their Own Names After Marriage,* includes a thorough review of all aspects of the name-change issue. It is available . . . from the Center for a Woman's Own Name, Barrington, Illinois.

The center is located in the suburban home of Terri P. Tepper, thirty-one, who went through court in Chicago two years ago, even though it wasn't legally necessary, to have her maiden name restored. ("There was no precedent," she explained.) Her case was handled by her husband, Lawrence Weiner, a lawyer.

"It just had to do with identity," Miss Tepper said recently. "I was Terri Tepper for twenty-two years. I had gone to college, graduated, and been an elementary school teacher, and all of a sudden I was out of the phone book and off the mailbox. All of a sudden, I felt my identity was buried."

Miss Tepper, who founded the nonprofit center in February 1973, said she now had 115 contacts throughout the country who disseminate information to women who want to use their own name.

The center's three directors are Miss Tepper; Priscilla Ruth MacDougall, a Wisconsin lawyer who is considered one of the country's leading authorities on the name-change issue; and Diana Altman, who founded the Name-Change group in Massachusetts, and who also happens to be Miss Tepper's cousin. . . . Tepper said her two children have been given her maiden name as their middle name: Nona Tepper Weiner, 7, and Jordan Tepper Weiner, 6.

Has she had any problems at all in her maiden name struggle? "Well, my in-laws were very much concerned about the issue," she replied. "My mother-in-law feels I'm breaking up homes by doing it."

This alleged violation of the sanctity of the family is often the traditionalists' major criticism of the use of maiden names, along with the resulting "embarrassment" it supposedly causes husbands and children. Advocates of maiden names argue that the high United States divorce

rate hardly suggests that using the husband's name pre-
serves the sanctity of the family.

Many Employers Reluctant

Several other women who were interviewed reported
instances of discrimination because they chose to use their
maiden names. Their examples ranged from employers
who refused to go along with a name change because it
complicated their record-keeping, to difficulty obtaining
credit cards, to hassles with clerks at state agencies who
were unaware of women's name rights.

And in Milwaukee last year [1973], a circut court judge
ruled that a married teacher could not legally resume her
maiden name—even though Wisconsin has no law prohibiting a married woman from using her birth name. The
case is being appealed to the State Supreme Court.

Linda Fosburg, thirty-one, a former executive director
of Citizens for Clean Air, Inc., said her husband, Lewis
Lloyd, always introduced her as "My wife, Linda Fosburg,"
and calls her "Fos," or "Fossie." She wears no wedding
ring, and there are two names, Fosburg and Lloyd, on the
mailbox of their . . . apartment.

In fact, the only people who have refused to accept her
maiden name are some of her friends. "They sometimes
refuse to go along with it," she said, sounding puzzled.
"They call me Linda Lloyd. They have a need to think of
me as married to Lewis."

Although the retention of one's maiden name is generally associated with feminism, many feminists eschew the
practice because, as they are quick to point out, the maiden
name is just another man's surname—that of the woman's
father.

As a result, some feminists are using their mother's
given name and adding the suffix, child. For example, a
woman named Ann Jones, the daughter of Helen Jones,
would become Ann Helenchild. Other women, such as

Laura X, founder of a library of women's history in Berkeley, California, are taking entirely new surnames in protest against being forced to use men's surnames.

"Almost every woman I know seems to be changing her name to one thing or another," said Diana Altman, thirty-two, the founder of Name-Change. "When I first did it, my mother said I would always be Mrs. Siegel to her. Now she's thinking about changing her name. So is my eighty-year-old grandmother. She says she'll never take a man's name again."

CHOOSING EQUALITY [4]

To make marriage equal is not to reverse the roles. It is to develop a new kind of marriage, one in which no one is the *head* of the household, and new ways of relating to each other must be learned.

To be honest, men do lose a few privileges when they become partners in marriage instead of boss of the family, though many of these "privileges" aren't as valuable as they might once have seemed.

What does a man have to lose?

1. If you are the kind of man who expects to come home every evening to a meal cooked by your wife and a house cleaned by her, no matter how busy she may be with her job or other activities, then you will find you must share the responsibilities of preparing the meals and cleaning the house.

2. If you are the kind of father who expects to have the children kept out of your way when you come home from work until you rest and then play with them a short time until your wife puts them to bed, you will find yourself much more involved in child care.

[4] From *Equal Marriage*, by Jean Stapleton and Richard Bright. Abingdon. '76. p22-35. Copyright © 1976 by Abingdon. Used by permission. Jean Stapleton is head of the journalism department at East Los Angeles College; Richard Bright is a marriage, family, and child counselor. They are wife and husband.

3. If you have expected to have the last say on family finances, choice of where to live and in what style, or how the family spends its leisure time, you will find that you will *share* those decisions.

4. If you believe a man must be tough, decisive, unemotional, aloof from domestic affairs, and always right in his decisions, you will be changing your concept of masculinity.

5. If you have always considered it your prerogative to spend most evenings and weekends on yourself, watching football or reading or pursuing a hobby, you will find that you spend more of your time sharing household and child-rearing chores. And your wife will have a bit more free time, which she may want to spend with you.

6. If you are the kind of man who expects many personal favors from your wife as a matter of course, you will have to stop thinking of her as your personal servant. She will no longer shuffle off to the kitchen obediently if you yell orders at her like Archie Bunker's "Bring me a beer, Edith."

7. If you are confident that you know exactly how life should be and have been living as though your marriage were a script handed to you by your parents or your peer group, you will lose the security of living predictably. In an equal marriage, you don't know how to behave in every situation, and you have to work out situations with logic or by trying different behaviors until you find one that is comfortable.

Interestingly, most of these "losses" are just the reverse side of what men have to gain from equal marriage:

1. In sharing the household and child-care tasks, you become a real partner to your wife, and you will have a better relationship. Two equals may share their lives, thoughts, and emotions freely. In contrast, an authoritarian husband would have to hide any anxiety or indecisiveness, while a subordinate wife would have to hide any activities and thoughts she thought the "boss" would not approve.

2. In sharing child care, you develop a real relationship with your children, one in which the children are not trying to impress Father or evade his punishment but one in which they know him as a person and feel comfortable confiding in him. Such a father will have real influence in guiding his children through the experiences of childhood and adolescence.

3. Just as you will be sharing more of the burdens of housekeeping and child-rearing, your wife will be able to share the burden of earning a living, taking the pressure off you. Whether and how much she works is an individual couple's decision, just as it is the couple's decision whether the husband will work and how much. . . .

4. If you stop defining masculinity in the traditional way, you will be free to do things once considered feminine without feeling threatened. Many men enjoy cooking and child care; football star Rosey Grier has even had the courage to take up needlepoint. None of the men reports any ill effects. Under the old definition of masculinity, men would have to forgo such enjoyable activities, at great loss to themselves. You will also be free to admit to not knowing everything, to not being sure about every decision, and you will be able to express emotions other than anger and pride. Likewise, you may be surprised to find your wife learning to do things once considered masculine, such as household repairs and understanding the stock market, and not being any less sexy for her new abilities.

5. You will discover that being born male and growing up makes you a man. You won't have to waste your life proving your manhood by conquering women or performing acts of bravado or drinking too much or being violent, ways that many men, such as the late Ernest Hemingway, have used to convince themselves that they really are men.

6. You may gain the companionship of your wife for those interests you have in common, now that you are shar-

ing the chores and she has a little more free time. You may discover that she loves football, too, or that your fishing trips can be combined with her rock-hounding.

7. You won't have to feel guilty about your wife's giving up a promising career for you. If she gives it up it will be because she wanted to or she was not as successful as she expected to be; if she decides to pursue it, both the decision and the success will have been hers, but you can have the same pride in her work as she has in yours.

8. You will gain an interesting companion (or keep one) as your wife takes on outside interests and grows as a person. You won't find yourselves, as so many married couples do, sitting across the table from each other at a restaurant and looking bored because you have nothing to say to each other. The conversation and the companionship will remain lively, something you'll remain eager to return to each day.

Some men will probably think that they have a right to feel superior to their wives because the wife *is* inferior. Psychological studies have shown that to be a rarity. A couple may not be equal in intelligence, but the less intelligent person may have more social ability or more creativity. The couple may not be equally attractive, but the less attractive person will have money or a prized quality to make up for it. . . .

Women, too, have a few things to lose in having an equal marriage though, again, these seem less like "privileges" when they are looked at more closely.

1. If you are the kind of woman who looks upon your husband as a meal ticket, a provider of goodies, you will have to realize that you too are capable of providing. You may need to go back to school or update your skills in order to be employable. But you will have to realize that your husband may not always be there, that he may need or want a chance to go back to school or stay out of work for a while for some other reason, that he could be inca-

pacitated, or that you may be able to make the difference between just getting by and being comfortable, and that the whole family is suffering by your not taking a job.

2. If you like the feeling of being the hub of the family, the "queen mother," you will have to be ready to share that central position with your husband as he develops close relationships with the children and shares in their care.

3. If you have enjoyed the position of having your husband make all the decisions while you blame him for anything that goes wrong, you will have to get used to sharing the responsibility for your joint decisions.

4. If you are used to winning arguments or getting your way by being emotional, you will have to start being straight about saying what you want and be prepared to give good reasons for it without getting overemotional.

5. If you usually get your husband or some other man to do all the heavy, dirty, or mechanical work on the grounds that you are too weak, dainty, and incompetent to do it because you are a woman, you may have to learn to carry your share of the load to the limit of your physical ability.

6. If you want to be placed on a pedestal and looked up to simply because you are a woman, you'll have to get used to being treated as a person and not having the one-up position occasionally as a compensation for your usual one-down position.

7. You, too, will have to get used to an unpredictable life in which you and your husband work out your tasks, your plans, your goals together instead of accepting them secondhand from television shows or your friends and family.

Of course, for women too these "losses" are just the reverse side of what you have to gain:

1. In sharing the breadwinning or being prepared to do so, you will also share the rewards and pleasures which

can come from having a job: you can enjoy an increased income; and, even if you never work at an income-producing job but are always prepared, you will have the security of knowing that you will not starve if something happens to your husband.

2. In sharing household chores and child care with your husband, you will have more free time to spend with your husband or to use in other involvements. You will find that your children are more emotionally healthy for having two parents who are not overburdened with child care but who both are involved with the children.

3. By sharing decision-making, you will find that you have a sense of being in control of your life, that you will not build up resentment against your husband for decisions that do not go right, since you shared in making the decisions.

4. By asking for what you want in a straight way and by not getting your way or winning arguments with emotionalism, you will have greater respect for yourself.

5. In developing your strength and competence with mechanical things, you will feel more secure when your husband is not available or if something should happen to him, and you will gain further self-respect the more you can do things for yourself.

6. If you leave the pedestal, you will know you are respected for yourself and not for your sex alone. You will no longer be patronized by being allowed on the pedestal in public and on Mother's Day while being kept in a one-down position most of the time.

7. You have the choice of whether to work so that if you choose to be a full-time homemaker and mother, you will not have been forced into the role but will have chosen it freely and so will not resent it.

8. You are more likely to enjoy your children as individuals if they are not your responsibility solely and if they are not the only source of your fulfillment.

9. If you work outside you will no longer have to feel responsible for doing a second full-time job as homemaker when you return from your paying job.

10. When you give up the security of a predictable life, you too will find that your marriage and your life are adventures, that both you and your husband will be more creative and will inspire each other to lead more creative lives.

By choosing to have an equal marriage, parents also gain an additional benefit for their children.

You'll have the satisfaction of knowing that you are giving your daughters and sons their full humanity, without limitations according to sex. . . .

There are also a few things many people fear they will lose in an equal marriage which they will not lose:

1. Their masculinity or femininity, though it will remain intact, will be redefined.

2. Their sexuality will not disappear. Although *Esquire* and other magazines have blamed an "epidemic" of impotence on liberated women, there has been no proof that impotence is becoming more common or that it is due to women's gaining equality. Impotence often may be a problem within a couple's relationship, but Masters and Johnson and others have found that it is most often caused by the man's having too high an expectation of himself. Some unliberated men may be threatened by liberated women and thus doubt their own potency, but men who are liberated from the straight jacket of prescribed masculine behavior will be complimented rather than threatened if a woman initiates sex or if she enjoys it, and they will not feel pressured to a superhuman performance, as demanded by the masculine mystique.

It's a toss-up what is supposed to happen to women's sexuality when marriage becomes equal and they have a choice in the matter. . . .

The reality is that some women might choose to have more and some women less sex if given an opportunity to tell their husbands what they want. Either way, it would be better sex, being voluntary, with women being free to express themselves and to take some of the initiative.

3. Men's status will not be lowered by having a wife who is an equal. Most people are impressed with a two-profession family. If not, then they will probably be impressed with the material goods two incomes can provide. If a wife is not working but the husband shares the evening and weekend household duties, most people will think highly of him for being a considerate husband, even if they do not understand that the work is equally his. . . .

What if a man is working full time and the wife is a full-time housewife? Can't he then feel justified in letting her do all the household chores and child care as part of her job since he does his job of bringing home the money?

According to the U.S. government, a housewife works ninety hours a week. Sometimes it is hard to see that she has been working all day, since much of her work is undone by the cooking of the next meal or by messy children. Some of her tasks don't show, like chauffeuring children, answering the telephone, and listening to the children's problems. Others are taken for granted, like shopping for groceries. But it all adds up to a workweek that is more than twice as long as the average paid worker's.

You really have a choice of either watching your wife put in the equivalent of another workweek while you are at home or sharing the load to get it done in half the time and being able to do things together.

It all boils down to rethinking the purpose of marriage. If your reason for getting married is to have your clothes washed, as well as having someone to wait on you and provide sex when you want it, then you are hiring a servant. Most of those services can be contracted for outside of marriage at a higher cost ($790 a month, the government estimates), but it is more honest than marrying a woman to make her a servant.

Few women these days will agree to such a utilitarian

marriage—few have to sell themselves into bondage just to survive. Most people now marry because they enjoy each other's company and want to be together and to raise a family together. Such a marriage of friends becomes a utilitarian exchange of services for financial support only gradually, after the first child is born and/or the couple's interests grow in different directions. When people decide for equality in marriage, they are asking to reverse that process or to prevent it from ever happening. Marriage is humanity's best refuge from loneliness, but only if it is a true partnership.

IV. MARRIED AND WORKING LIFE

EDITOR'S INTRODUCTION

This section examines some of the old patterns and new directions as they affect men as well as women in family life and in careers. For a man to be constricted by cultural conditioning is as self-inhibiting as it is for a woman. A man is expected always to be strong, impervious to pain and especially to emotional stress, dominant in the role of lord and master; a woman is expected to be docile, submissive, passive, fulfilled in the role of subordinate. In contrast, opponents of fixed roles insist upon individual freedom of choice and shared family responsibilities. They emphasize the importance of fathers as nurturing parents caring for very young children, an emphasis that creates self-esteem, provides good models for growing children, and enhances family life.

Overcoming the traditional assumptions of our society, however, presents serious problems, and both men and women encounter difficulties. Women frequently have trouble developing a strong self-image and a positive expectation of success in the world of work. Men, on the other hand, are frequently unable to admit emotional difficulties and to ask for help. A number of the articles in this section are concerned with these aspects of self-perception and self-deception.

Several excerpts have to do with recent successes in narrowing the odds against one sex or the other. One such change was a court decision granting widowers the same Social Security benefits as widows. Another advance discussed is the ordination of women as priests and ministers by churches that have traditionally barred them. Countering this trend is the surprising rejection of Equal Rights Amendments to state constitutions in New York and New

Jersey after the voters in those states had approved the same amendment to the United States Constitution.

Sexism can be subtle or blatant. An article by Carol Christ analyzing the popular television characters Archie Bunker and Marcus Welby makes clear how pervasive and ingrained are our traditional concepts and how, consciously or not, we accept them.

SOCIAL SECURITY AND EQUAL RIGHTS [1]

The Supreme Court March 19 [1975] unanimously struck down as unconstitutional a part of the Social Security law that provided survivors' benefits for widows with children but denied them to widowers in the same situation. The section of the Social Security Act mandating different treatment for men and women, the court said, "unjustifiably discriminated against women wage earners by affording them less protection for their survivors than is provided to male employes." Although that section had been part of federal law since 1939, wrote Justice William J. Brennan Jr., it was based on an assumption "that could not be tolerated under the Constitution": while the earnings of men are "vital to the support of their families," women's earnings "do not significantly contribute to their families' support."

Stephen C. Wiesenfeld, a New Jersey widower, had filed suit (*Weinberger* v. *Wiesenfeld*) after his wife Paula died in childbirth, leaving him with an infant son to support. Mrs. Wiesenfeld's contributions to the Social Security fund were based on her $10,000 annual income. Mr. Wiesenfeld had been earning $2,000-$3,000. When he applied for social security benefits, he was told that his son was eligible, but that only widows were entitled to benefits for themselves.

The Supreme Court upheld the federal district court's

[1] From "Supreme Court Ends Discrimination Between Social Security Benefits." *Editorials on File.* 6:384+. Ap. 1-15, 75. Reprinted with permission from *Editorials on File.* © 1975 Facts on File, Inc.

ruling that the discrimination between widows and widowers was unconstitutional. Justice Brennan observed that the survivors' benefits had been added to the Social Security law to allow a parent to stay home to take care of children when the major wage earner had died.

The Arizona Republic

(Editorial, March 26, 1975, Phoenix)

When the Supreme Court struck down as unconstitutional a provision of the Social Security law denying survivors' benefits to widowers with children, it paradoxically struck a blow for equal rights for women.

At the same time, it demonstrated once again that women don't need the Equal Rights Amendment to protect them against discrimination.

The case involved Stephen C. Wiesenfeld, a self-employed consultant, whose income runs to between $2,000 and $3,000 a year.

In 1970, Wiesenfeld married Paula Polatschek, a schoolteacher. Although they soon had a child, Jason, she continued to work, earning about $10,000 a year.

In 1972, Mrs. Wiesenfeld died in childbirth. Wiesenfeld applied for survivors' benefits for himself and Jason. He was granted the benefits for Jason but not for himself.

Under the law, he was told, only widows could receive such benefits for themselves.

Wiesenfeld filed suit in Federal District Court, arguing that he was being deprived of his constitutional guarantees of due process and equal protection of the laws. A three-judge panel ruled in his favor, and the Supreme Court unanimously upheld the ruling.

Writing for the court, Associate Justice William J. Brennan Jr. said it was unconstitutional to assume that "male workers' earnings are vital to the support of their families, while the earnings of female workers do not significantly contribute to their families' support."

Mrs. Wiesenfeld had paid the same Social Security taxes as a man but had been denied the same protection for her family after her death that a male worker would have received, Justice Brennan declared.

The effect of the decision was to open the way to challenge all laws discriminating against either men or women on the basis of sex.

Wiesenfeld's victory thus was a victory for women's lib.

Post-Tribune

(Editorial, March 23, 1975, Gary, Indiana)
Reprinted from the Gary, Indiana, *Post-Tribune* by permission.

Whatever the various remaining legislatures may do, . . . the United States Supreme Court has taken a long step toward ratifying at least the concept of the so-called Equal Rights Amendment (ERA) to the United States Constitution.

That amendment merely states that there shall be no discrimination by law because of sex.

It has been generally regarded as a "women's rights" amendment. The fact, however, that the case decided . . . [March 19, 1975] established by a unanimous court the right of a widower to the same Social Security benefits accorded a widow does not alter the basic concept.

There are other ways in which men are denied full equality. Some states, for example, allow alimony payments in divorce cases only to women.

With our changing lifestyle, it seems inevitable that there will be a number of families in which the wife is the larger breadwinner. That was an issue in . . . [the] case involving Social Security help for rearing a minor child. It would also be an issue in challenges to the male alimony ban.

Those who have done more legal research on the issue indicate that there are more laws which discriminate against women than against men. That would seem likely since up until recently, at least, men have had the larger voice in making the laws.

But the court has now held that sex should not be the basis of deciding such issues.

That may make the ERA unnecessary. We still believe, though, that it would make more sense to have the point spelled out among our basic rights.

MEN AND EMOTIONAL PROBLEMS [2]

It was obvious that Frank Johnson (the name is fictitious) was having troubles. He'd quit three jobs in a little over two years. His home life had deteriorated: he had become so snappish with the children that they were avoiding him, and on several occasions he had blown up at his wife in public. But when his closest friend said something to Frank about getting help, he blew up at the friend, too.

"Look," he shouted, "I can take care of myself!"

But the fact was that he couldn't. Within six months, his wife had moved out, taking the children; and Frank, depressed and harassed, was about to lose another job.

Frank Johnson's problems were particular to him, but his flat refusal to get help was absolutely typical of most troubled men. They are plain scared of telling their troubles to a marriage counselor, psychologist, minister or family doctor. A man will consult with a mechanic about his car, or get advice from a neighbor about his lawn; but when it comes to the things at the absolute center of his existence, like his mental and emotional health, four times out of five he will refuse to consult expert help. As a result, uncountable millions of American males are muddling along unhappily in jobs they don't like, living in cold, dis-

[2] Article entitled "Why Men Won't Seek Help," by James Lincoln Collier, free-lance writer. *Reader's Digest.* 107:138-41. S. '75. Reprinted with permission from the September 1975 *Reader's Digest.* Copyright 1975 by The Reader's Digest Association, Inc.

tant marriages, losing contact with their children—in short, putting up with situations that they often could change with professional aid.

Michael Peter, staff psychologist at the State University of New York at Binghamton, reports: "Fifty-five percent of the students here are male, but more than 60 percent of the people who come in to see us with problems are women." Mark Kane Goldstein, a Gainesville, Florida, Veterans Administration Hospital psychologist specializing in family work, reports that "over two thirds of our applications for treatment were initiated by wives." Says Sanford Sherman, executive director of the Jewish Family Service of New York, "Four out of five times it's the wife who comes in to see us first."

Today, adds Sherman, "Men in America feel that they ought to be able to deal with anything that comes along, and it's an admission of failure if they're having trouble." Some men would rather fail at their marriage or with their children than admit that something is wrong and seek a solution.

In one case, a father had a sixteen-year-old son who came to him several times, saying, "Dad, I feel lousy all the time." The fact that the boy would open up like this ought to have warned the father that something was seriously awry. But the father could not admit that there might be something wrong; that would have been an admission that he had "failed" as a father. So he would only respond, "Oh, it's a stage that teen-agers go through."

Six months later, the youngster experimented with LSD and had a dangerously bad experience, missing two weeks of school. Fortunately, a school psychiatrist insisted that the boy get therapy, and the story had a happy ending: a year later, he graduated from high school with a fine academic record. But what pain son and father could have been spared had the father at the outset got the help that the boy obviously wanted.

Another deep-seated attitude American men have is what the Spanish call *machismo*, or manliness. This ideal has come to mean that a man must always be a tower of male strength, and that he must never demonstrate any feminine "weaknesses."

A classic illustration of the troubles caused by *machismo* is provided by a husband we'll call Bill Dodge. Most men suffer occasionally from sexual failure due to fatigue, liquor or worry. But Bill did not realize that an occasional lapse isn't anything to worry about. The first time it happened to him he was shocked at this sign of "unmanliness," and soon he was caught up in a spiral: each failure simply increased his anxieties, making the next failure all the more likely. Finally, he withdrew from sex altogether. His wife suggested that he "see the doctor," but he refused. "There's nothing wrong with me," he insisted. "I've just been working too hard lately."

Normally, a problem such as Bill's can be treated fairly quickly by an experienced counselor. But Bill could not bring himself to get help, to admit that there was something wrong with him.

There is yet another aspect to this concept of how an American male is taught to think, feel and act. Most men are afraid of being expressive, of saying what they feel. Says marriage specialist Goldstein, "Men aren't supposed to have sensitive, warm feelings or feelings of tenderness for the people around them—much less express them." It is like the story of the old Vermont farmer forty years married, who said, "I love Sarah Jane so much that sometimes it's all I can do to keep from telling her."

Jack O. Balswick, professor of sociology at the University of Georgia, has studied this phenomenon carefully. He says,

In learning to be a man, the boy in American society comes to value indications of masculinity expressed largely through physical courage, toughness, competitiveness and aggressiveness.

Femininity is, in contrast, expressed largely through gentleness and responsiveness. Parents teach their sons that a real man does not show his emotions.

Once a boy is trained to believe that he shouldn't let people know what he is feeling, it is not easy for him to change. And inevitably, if a man has troubles even expressing his feelings to his family, he'll avoid going to a therapist or counselor. How, then, can men who need help be persuaded to seek it?

Family counselors essentially agree that men will accept help in the right circumstances. One of those circumstances is a willingness for those involved with the troubled man to understand that problems between people are rarely one person's "fault," if indeed they can be said to be anybody's fault.

Most of the problems we see [says counselor Sherman] are not a question of something the husband is doing, or the wife, or the kids, but a family affair. Everybody is contributing, whatever the trouble is, and everybody's involved in it. We begin from this point. Even when a wife contacts us first, if you get hold of the husband, you find that nine times out of ten he does want to come in.

Most experts in the field agree that it is vastly preferable for a counselor to deal with *both* husband and wife, and some flatly insist that both *must* be seen.

Strangely enough, a wife often contributes to a problem by accepting the *machismo* idea herself. Says Sherman,

Many wives believe that men are supposed to be moral and physical bulwarks on which they can lean. When a wife takes this for granted, she is reinforcing the male in the same idea. She may rail at him for not being more tender and expressive, or for not being willing to get some help for a family problem—at the same time she's supporting the *machismo* ideal of never admitting to human frailties.

Everybody involved has to work on emotional problems together. And anybody who is involved with a male having problems should start by indicating a willingness to seek counseling, too. Says Sherman,

> A wife shouldn't say, "There's something wrong with you; you need help." What she can say is, "I want to see somebody, and I want you to come, too, for our sakes." By asking him to come for both their sakes—not because he "needs help"—she allows him a way to see somebody without putting the sole onus on himself.

There has never lived a human being who didn't from time to time need somebody's help. Most American males are proud of their masculinity; but in teaching them, as we do, that they must always be strong, and never show the weaknesses that all of us possess, we put a terrible burden on them. It is one that few people can successfully bear.

Today, men are just starting to learn that perhaps it won't hurt them to admit to a failing now and again. Says Sherman, "Sure, four out of five times it's the wife who comes in first—but ten years ago it would have been nine times out of ten." Still, for most men, getting counseling is difficult, even demeaning. To get help, they need the help of those around them who care for them.

WOMEN AND JOBS [3]

Helen Shadduck, a thirty-five-year-old California mother whose four children range in age from eleven to fifteen, decided to go back to work as a bookkeeper recently after fifteen years at home.

> My husband earns a good salary [she said], but because of inflation it's tough to get ahead on one salary.
> Besides, after staying home with four kids for twenty-four hours a day, I wanted some adult companionship, a feeling of accomplishment; having the cleanest floor on the block isn't the greatest thing that can happen to you.

[3] Article entitled "Women Entering Job Market at an 'Extraordinary Pace.'" by Robert Lindsey, staff correspondent. New York *Times.* p 1. S. 12, '76. Copyright © 1976 by The New York Times Company. Reprinted by permission.

In taking a job, Mrs. Shadduck joined an avalanche of women pouring into the nation's work force this year that is not only shaping up as a tide of enormous proportions, but depriving the Ford Administration of what had promised to be one of its hottest issues in November [1976]— a declining unemployment rate.

Money is important, says Anne Gordon, a thirty-eight-year-old mother of three who recently went to work as a librarian for the Battery Park City Authority in Manhattan after sixteen years of rearing children. But, she said, a sense of pride and accomplishment are also important. "Someone is saying, 'Here's what you're worth,' " she said.

June Barlow, another New York City woman who recently returned to work, said: "Women's lib gave me the impetus to get out of the house; it helped me to get out and start looking and getting back into the big world."

The number of American women who work outside their homes has been rising since 1947. But during the last two years, and especially in 1976, women have entered the job market at a pace called "extraordinary" by Alan Greenspan, chairman of the President's Council of Economic Advisers.

Eli Ginzburg, a Columbia University economist and chairman of the National Commission for Manpower Policy, calls the flood of women into the work force "the single most outstanding phenomena of our century."

"Its long-term implications are absolutely unchartable, in my opinion," he said. "It will affect women, men and children, and the cumulative consequences of that will only be revealed in the 21st and 22d centuries." . . .

Pattern Seen in Statistics

The following United States Department of Labor statistics illustrate the pattern:

☐ During the last five months there has been a net increase of more than 1.1 million women over sixteen who have taken jobs or begun seeking work, swelling the nation's total female work force to 38.8 million. Most of the newcomers are in the twenty-five to forty-four age group, women who in the past have tended to stay at home and raise children.

☐ During the last twenty-four months, the number of women in the work force has increased by 2.8 million, accounting for two thirds of the increase in the nation's work force, and almost 30 percent of the increase in the last twelve months.

☐ Women, who comprised 33 percent of the national labor force in 1960, and 38.1 percent in 1970, now account for 40.7 percent, a proportion that was not expected to be reached until 1985 by Labor Department forecasters as recently as . . . [1973].

☐ Almost 48 percent of American women over sixteen years of age now work or want a job, a figure that has risen a full percentage point since last spring [1976] and compares with 43.2 percent in 1970. Some economists say it is possible that half of American women over sixteen will be in the work force within two or three years.

The reasons for this broad change appear to be complex and not fully understood. But interviews with scores of women in twelve different regions of the country disclosed some of the reasons.

In addition to the growing number of young single women looking for their first jobs, as well as newly divorced women who have little or no income from their former husbands, there are women whose husbands earn less than $10,000 a year and a second salary, because of inflation, is often virtually necessary for survival.

There are the wives of middle-income husbands whose paychecks permit the family in an inflationary period to maintain its standard of living. The incomes of these families range from about $10,000 to $15,000 annually.

A third group is made up of women from higher income

families whose desire for broader horizons, rather than money, is the primary reason for working.

Roots of the Force

The roots of the expanding female work force, according to interviews with labor experts and newly working women, began in the 1960s with the economic liberation of young wives, which was aided by effective birth control methods and spurred by inflation.

But the interviews indicated there were other significant factors: a rising divorce rate; an increasing number of female college graduates who want careers; the psychological climate induced by publicity over the women's movement that makes it more socially acceptable for young mothers to work, encourages more older women to work, and has reduced housewives' self-esteem; federal laws that have increased hiring opportunities for women; and an increasing number of counseling centers that help prepare women for jobs.

In Rochester, New York, Mary Ann Berdych, forty years old, a mother of five, reentered the job market after fourteen years because of a divorce, and says it was purely for economic reasons. "I had to unless I didn't want to eat," she said.

In Minneapolis, Mia Firefile, a twenty-six-year-old mother of three, got a clerical job after her husband left her. "I guess women's lib had something to do with it. I sure don't let no man push me around," she said.

In New Orleans, Shirley Adams, forty-nine, went to work to pay for the rising costs of sending her two daughters to college. In Washington, Rita Laccetti, the wife of a career military officer, took a job at a new Bloomingdale's store there simply to have something interesting to do. And in South Orange, New Jersey, Mary Gotsill, the wife of a high school coach, went to work in a university library "not for the money, but for me."

President Ford has never met Mrs. Gotsill, Mrs. Adams, Mrs. Laccetti, nor any of the other women who have swollen the nation's labor force recently. But their decisions to return to work have torpedoed his Administration's forecasts of a leveling off of the nation's unemployment rate at 7 percent by the end of this year, and indirectly, given some campaign ammunition to his Democratic opponent, Jimmy Carter.

In August [1976], the unemployment rate for the once typical American wage earner—married men—declined to 4.2 percent from 4.5 percent, reaching a level that economists not long ago regarded as theoretically close to "full employment."

But, despite Administration claims of a continuing, vigorous economic recovery, the overall national unemployment figure edged up to 7.9 percent last month [August 1976], the third consecutive monthly increase.

More Americans than ever now have jobs—almost 88 million. But the fact that more and more people—particularly women, but also teen-agers—are seeking jobs means that the politically significant unemployment rate can't be lowered proportionately.

The August labor figures indicated that many of the women who had decided to work were not finding jobs. The national unemployment rate for men in August was 7 percent; it was 9.1 percent for women.

Conversations with women who recently went back to work indicated that many of them had enjoyed new experiences and found broader horizons and opportunities than they had had at home.

Nancy Niehaus, thirty-three, who works as a school publicist in Minneapolis, said: "I really went to work to see if I could earn a high enough wage to get a divorce and support my boys." But, she said, "The job saved my marriage. My husband treats me like a different person; we found mutual interests and became good friends once more."

THE FEAR OF SUCCESS [4]

Are women their own worst friends in the business world? Ever since Matina Horner's famous 1968 study revealed that some women actually *fear* success, social scientists have been trying to determine what factors in the female personality impede her climb up the ladder to success. . . . [In the spring of 1976] some subtle but important impediments to feminine advancement were described at two sessions of the Eastern Psychological Association meeting in New York City.

In one session, Toni Falbo of Wake Forest University (Winston-Salem, North Carolina) presented results of a study involving 226 male and female undergraduates who were asked to comment on success and failure.

"If a woman was presented as succeeding in a task usually performed by males, men and women tended to say: 'She was lucky, she worked hard,'" reported Falbo. "But if a successful male is so presented, they say he is 'capable.' When women and men describe their own success, they do the same thing." The fact that women attribute their success to an unstable cause such as luck implies it will not continue, Falbo believes.

"But when it comes to their own personal failure, males attribute it to "bad luck," Falbo found, while women say: "I'm incapable."

"Men have a way of explaining failure that makes it less ego defeating," she commented.

In other words, men tend to blame their failures on outside influences (over which they have no control). Women accept failure as a result of their own inadequacies.

A study of eighty Vanier College (Montreal, Canada) students presented at the same session supported Falbo's results. Coralyn Fontaine of Vanier found females with the

[4] Article entitled "Women Are Their Own Worst Friends." *Science Digest.* 80:8-9. Ag. '76. Reprinted with permission of *Science Digest.* Copyright © 1976 The Hearst Corporation.

highest desire to achieve experienced the lowest amount of pride after failing an anagram test. Males with the highest desire to achieve, however, retained a high amount of pride after failure. "High achieving females also felt more shame than males after failure," said Fontaine.

In reality, she explained, the test was rigged so no one actually succeeded or failed. But, when female high-achievers were told by experimenters that they had failed the test and had to select another, they picked the one supposedly requiring the least ability. High achieving males who had been told they failed picked the test requiring the greatest ability.

Another key factor that may play a role in success or failure for women is early choice of career, according to a paper presented by Jeanne Marecek later in the session. In a group of fifty Swarthmore College (Swarthmore, Pennsylvania) alumni who graduated in the early 1970s, women showed more uncertainty than men in choice of careers, in spite of the fact that all the women but one expected to be working at age thirty-five. One factor that helps females make an early career choice is a mother who works, Marecek noted. (While she was talking, an elderly woman in the largely female audience got up and tried to open a heavy window behind the speakers. A young man sitting in the seat nearest the window went to her aid. There was a ripple of good-natured laughter.)

In an earlier session, the current theory that black women do not have the same fear of success as white women was challenged by Jacqueline Fleming of the Radcliffe Institute. Fleming, who is black, found that in two out of three studies she conducted with high school and college students, black women avoided behavior that would lead to success.

"How do you spend your time?" read one of the questions. "Resting" was the favorite answer. Fleming's conclusion: "The work orientation of black women, which is probably the fruit of necessity, has been confused with achievement motivation."

Between presentations, Barbara Richardson, of Cornell University, who served as chairperson, commented: "I keep coming across this lower pride on the part of women. It's rather sad. Why?" The papers offered no answer but as Richardson pointed out later, they are steps on the way to "bigger and better theories with regard to women."

WOMEN IN BUSINESS ADMINISTRATION [5]

Reprinted from *U.S. News & World Report*.

Dr. Greiff, are more women now seeking careers in business management—and are you finding that they are as well qualified as men?

More and more women are seeking careers in all sorts of specialties—in medicine, in law, in dentistry and certainly in the business field.

As for the second part of your question, keep in mind that women have managed all their lives. They've managed businesses, their families, their homes, and they've managed many other things for which they've not received adequate credit. Management is a field in which they've done quite well, and there's absolutely no question in my mind that they certainly can be as qualified as men.

Your question really almost doesn't have to be answered, except that many companies ask that question, too.

What's the best way for a woman to prepare herself for a business-management career?

There are four or five essential things a woman should do: (1) develop a keen sense of awareness regarding one's coping mechanisms under normal and stress circumstances; (2) obtain the best education, including if possible an MBA degree; (3) expose oneself to a number of situations and

[5] "How to Make the Most of Today's Opportunities," interview with Dr. Barrie Sanford Greiff, psychiatrist, lecturer in occupational psychiatry at Harvard University School of Business. *U.S. News & World Report*. 81:79-82. S. 27, '76.

develop a number of contacts in a variety of fields; (4) develop a strong sense of realism and perseverance, particularly with regard to the subtle pressures directed toward women.

When does that kind of preparation begin?
Immediately—and I mean that quite seriously. It has to develop in terms of somebody saying: "You can do anything you want if you're capable of doing it." That has to come from both father and mother.

We've traditionally thought of women as being weak, passive and dependent. That's a role stereotype. We have to think of women as individuals who have the same intellectual and motivational characteristics as men. The biological characteristics are different, but most of the other elements are socioculturally determined.

Are girls and young women finding more examples of successful women to emulate in business management?
Yes. More women are going back to work in the corporate field. Many after ages thirty to thirty-five are making the change from exclusive home responsibilities to working in business organizations. The schools are stressing such career paths, so that teen-age girls are getting a better idea of the opportunities open to them in the business fields.

Are business-administration schools opening their doors to women?
Absolutely, as evidenced by the increased enrollment of women at business schools in this country. Really, there's no choice: If they accept the fact that organizations are dynamic and not static, then they have to accept women, because that's what growing organizations require. Simmons College [in Boston] has developed specific MBA programs just for women.

Does the Harvard Business School offer special classes or special help for women?

There are people always available to give advice on a number of issues. I don't think there's a necessity for special classes for women. That would be a mistake because it would place them in an unnecessary, exclusive category.

How much has women's enrollment grown at the Harvard Business School?

Figures are not available, but there has been a significant increase in the past ten years.

Once a woman is in business school, should she take the same courses that a man in her specialty would take?

She should take every course she needs to make her an outstanding manager. Subject areas have no gender.

Some educators say that women need special counseling and education for the problems that women are going to run into in business and industry. Do you agree with that?

No. I think women should be aware, just as men should be aware, that there are unique problems that people run into in the business world.

For instance, most business schools give very little information about the human dilemmas men and women experience in business—the problems of traveling, of relocation, of job loss and job stress, etc.

Since 1970, I have taught a course at the Harvard Business School entitled "The Executive Family" which looks at these issues. But more schools should pay attention to such problems.

What do you discuss in this class?

Primarily we discuss the complex relationships between the individual, the family and the business organization.

We look at the trade-offs and the conflicts involved in dynamic married couples' lives.

For example, we examine the "dual-careers phenomenon," which I think is going to be the major factor altering the American family in the next twenty-five years. We look at the psychological and physical stress exerted on people who are actively engaged in the world of business. We focus on the effects of traveling, relocation and shifting priorities of organizations, etc.

Does this indicate that young people now training for careers are more conscious of problems involving family and company?

I think young people today are very sensitive to the quality of their lives. Whether they can translate that concern into action remains to be seen.

When push comes to shove, and people have to make critical decisions, sometimes their idealism changes. My experience with a lot of business people is that they play a waiting game: They say, "We'll postpone our personal and family needs now, and make them up later in our lives." That just doesn't work.

What do young people in management training look for most?

They look for opportunities that will provide personal and professional growth.

What disturbs them most?

I think they're concerned most about the trade-offs involved in their careers: how much time for personal needs and family needs versus organizational demands.

A major issue for young couples engaged in dual careers is whether or not to have children.

"Some Husbands Are Quite Jealous"

What about career conflicts between husband and wife?

A lot of men are quite interested in having their wives enter careers—that is, from a *theoretical* point of view. They look forward to the double income and to the reduction of pressure in their own lives in case they lose their job.

But there are certain problems they don't anticipate. For instance, if the wife is required to relocate and the husband is enjoying his present job, it produces a major conflict in their life. Also, some husbands are quite jealous, and fret when their wives are traveling alone.

For a woman, too, travel presents unique problems fostered by a society that has difficulty accepting the fact that women can function quite well on their own.

Do such problems tend to revive male chauvinism among "liberated" husbands of women executives?

Absolutely.

There's another situation that occurs at times: If the wife is traveling, friends of the husband may invite him over to dinner during her absence, and he may feel resentful and "infantilized." He may sense that others feel sorry for him and that they perceive him as not being able to take care of himself.

Then, of course, there's the problem of the wife who comes home in a fatigued state, with the subsequent unfavorable consequences leading to complications in the couple's social and sexual life.

Do you find that management students worry a great deal about the effect business obligations will have on their personal relationships?

I think so. Men have not been in a position in the past of having to share their wives with other men in the corporate world.

In the traditional scene, the wife has remained at home and primarily been in a female environment during the day—or her office career was that of secretary, which didn't have the same status as the corporate-executive woman.

Are male students forewarned that their wives might make more money than they do?
Some of them like the idea, and some of them are quite threatened by it. Certainly it's one of the issues that we talk about.

Has "women's liberation" been a help or a hindrance to business-oriented women?
It's a mixed bag in a way. There's no question that the "women's liberation" movement has helped awaken the consciousness of America to the fact that women have a capacity to deal with a number of complex business, political and economic issues.

When men become threatened, however, they talk of "women's lib" in a pejorative way. One reason is that their territory has been invaded. That is a fact. One of the things that is going to occur in this country is "job collision." By that I mean people are going to be colliding for jobs that were exclusively and primarily for the male.

Is that awareness found among business-school males when they start looking for jobs?
There's no question about that. Some of the male graduate students feel as though they're being moved aside because women have to be put in a particular job.

Are you saying that a kind of reverse discrimination goes on in the hiring of women graduates?
There might be reverse discrimination because of the fact that companies are under social, moral and legal pressure to hire more women. But rather than call it reverse

discrimination, it might be better to call it an effort to achieve a fair balance.

At the same time—and I really want to make this point—if a woman is going to enter the business world, then she's going to have to do all the things a man does.

Will the woman who enters the business world as an executive have to adopt some so-called masculine attitudes—become aggressive in her job?

Let me begin by stating that the word "aggression" is not exclusively a masculine word, nor does it imply negative qualities.

She's going to have to realize the trade-offs involved in a business career, including the enormous energy involved in business travel. In other words, she'll have to anticipate being challenged, criticized, condemned or refuted. I have seen many women who have not really been honest with themselves in the competitive business role. They have said, "We want all the benefits of our womanhood, but few of the problems of our male colleagues."

It's interesting to note that many men are very uncomfortable in challenging women in a similar way they would challenge men. Perhaps it's the man's upbringing, in which he incorporates values about women and subsequently treats them as precious, fragile—and inferior.

So women executives are learning the punishments as well as the rewards of a successful business career—

Yes, and in a variety of ways.

For instance, I think that as women move into the corporate world, they are subject to the same physical impairment that men are. Traditionally there's a lower incidence of coronary heart disease and ulcers in women.

I think we'll probably see more of the negative effects of stress on women, because you can't enter a competitive world and do all the things that competitive people do without experiencing some of the consequences. It's postulated that women's biological makeup has provided a protective mechanism against coronary heart disease. But we know that stress is a factor in this disorder; hence, I think we might see more of it in businesswomen.

Don't women have different emotional responses to job pressures than men?

Well, that's an interesting question. Several years ago, an article appeared in the New York *Times* written by a physician who said that women did not have the capacity to become President or hold major positions, primarily because their monthy periods subjected them to severe emotional swings.

I thought that statement was hogwash for a number of reasons: (1) While it's true a number of women might be affected by their menstrual periods, there is no major evidence to suggest faulty judgment or an inability to make major decisions during this period; and (2) with regard to being President, it's ironic that John F. Kennedy, while President of the United States, had been on a series of steroid hormones to control a major physical disorder. It is well known that among their many side effects these steroid hormones significantly affect one's mood—to the point, in large enough doses, that a psychotic process may occur, thereby affecting judgment and subsequent decision making.

Men don't have menstrual periods, but they certainly have mood swings during the month as a result of the weather, stress circumstances and other interpersonal conflicts.

Do women prefer to work for a man rather than a woman?

That depends, of course, on the women involved. Some women have felt that women make tougher bosses. Sometimes one sees a "queen-bee syndrome" among upper-level women executives trying to protect their status. In such a case they are less inclined to promote younger women.

This is not, however, exclusively a woman's problem because similar situations may occur with men. I don't think those feelings are unusual. We're really talking about the phenomena of competition, jealousy, maturity, etc.—factors present in both sexes.

Stereotypes of Woman Boss "A Myth"

Is the woman boss all the things some younger women think she's going to be?

How can she be? That depends on the fantasy/reality capacity of younger women. Many individuals seem to have a distorted image of the woman manager—e.g., tough, inconsiderate, threatened, hostile, etc. I think this stereotype, like many others, is a myth.

How about the woman who has had to battle her way through prejudice to reach her position, and so becomes intolerant of mistakes or laxity in other women?

She might be. But I say that depends on the woman rather than on her sex, because it's certainly true of the man also. Lots of men say, "I want this guy to work his behind off because that's the way I did it."

What should a management-trained woman look for in a prospective employer?

I think she should look for all the same things a man looks for: whether the job is interesting, provides advancement, gives adequate compensation, and what the trade-offs are. In addition, I think she should look for the sincerity of that organization in hiring and promoting various groups—women, blacks, etc.

But ultimately, I really believe, what's going to count is how she performs in that organization. If she performs well, most likely she'll advance. There are no guarantees, of course, for either sex, particularly in this day and age where so many variables determine the effect on one's career.

Suppose a company is not very forward-looking in its antidiscriminatory policy? Should a woman gamble and take a job there?

It depends upon what primarily motivates her to work for the company.

Lots of people start off working for a company mainly because it's a springboard for other organizations.

While getting a foothold in management, can women afford to take on marriage and family—or should those wait?

Well, can a man afford to take on the problems of management and family? Some can; others can't.

We have seen the family as primarily the responsibility of women, but it has to be looked at both ways. Can a woman afford to do it? Some women can. Some women like to do it, and some women decide that they want to postpone their careers.

I think that, whether a man or a woman, if you're going to have a family and a career, you'd better seriously think about what that involves—a great deal of juggling and trade-offs.

Yes, I think a woman can afford it—as much as a man can afford it.

When children enter the picture, is it a good time for a woman to quit working until the youngsters are in school?

You'd better plan to spend a reasonable amount of time with those children if you want them to get the benefits of early-life training—and I think early-life training is critical.

I don't think women have to quit work. There are lots of ways of handling it as long as parents remain involved with their children.

Will the growth of day care and nursery schools be a help to women executives?

Actually I'm very concerned about the growth of such institutions. It's very difficult to have large numbers of day care centers with qualified people taking care of children. Kids need love, consistency and trust, and those qualities usually come most effectively from the people who brought them into the world. I say "the people"—not just the mother, but the father too.

If people are planning ambitious careers, with each involved in traveling and a lot of time away from home, then they should seriously think twice about having any children in the early stages of their careers.

Will some women, after trying a management career, be happier in concentrating on family and children?

Undoubtedly. We've talked about career in terms of "jobs," but this in no way should minimize a career as a mother.

One of the problems of women going to work in organizations is that it has resulted in unnecessary guilt in women who really enjoy staying at home, raising a family and being housewives. And it has made many of them feel very inadequate. Many have gone back to work to compensate for their sense of guilt—which I think is a disaster, because they don't really want to take an outside job.

Sometimes they're pressured by a husband who says: "Look, I think you'll be more interesting if you go back to work, because you're becoming a bore at home." Then when wives go back to work, the husband comes home and asks: "Well, isn't my supper ready? What's wrong? How come the house is not as clean?" They've put their wives in the classic double-bind situation where, whatever the wives do, they lose—and ultimately, it's also the husband and family who will lose.

Therefore, I don't think a woman should ever go back to work unless she genuinely wants to go back to work.

Is it possible that sometime in years ahead we might find women business executives marrying "househusbands"?

You know, I've thought about that idea. Anthropologically speaking, there are certain tribes in which the women are the workers and the men remain at home. There is a precedent for that, but I don't see it happening in the next twenty-five or thirty or fifty years for a significant number of men.

Again, there's somewhat of a precedent in the kibbutz in Israel, where both men and women share both roles—outside jobs and work at home. It's possible that situation could develop here, providing there's a culture that allows it to develop. Maybe people who live in communes represent the prototypes of such future development.

Can the partners in a dual-career marriage attain true equality?

The odds tend to be stacked in favor of men—no question about it. But the pressure is also stacked on the man, too, and that's been minimized by the "women's liberation" movement.

If the man is the primary wage earner, he has the major responsibility of keeping that family economically afloat, of traveling and of maintaining the physical energy necessary at home and on the job. I think many women who are not involved in the world of business fail to see the anonymity, the loneliness or the boredom of going from city to city to city, and the amount of energy and restraint necessary for men away from home.

What personal qualities does a woman in business management need most in order to cope with these conflicts and pressures?

She needs, most of all, a good sense of self-esteem—a feeling that she's worth something. I think that's really fundamental. Everything else is secondary.

If she has a high sense of self-esteem and she believes what she's doing to be interesting and fair and honest, then in addition she needs all the other characteristics that any executive would need. These include analytic skills, good judgment, the ability to compromise and the ability to cope with losses or crises. She would need high energy levels and the capacity to relax. She would need a sense of humor—I think this is critical—and she would need the ability to maintain an over-all perspective of her limitations and the limitations of those around her.

How long will it be before women account for a significant proportion of top management in this country?
I think it will take many, many years. But there's no question: It's coming.

Within Twenty-five Years, a Woman President
Could a woman handle the job of being US President?
The answer is obvious: Absolutely yes. I would think that in the next quarter century we would have a woman as President. And why not? Exclusive male membership in major managerial roles is disappearing. You can't educate millions of women, admit them to major schools, create high expectations—and then squelch the whole thing at that point. This would result in tremendous frustration and subsequent human explosion.

Are there dangers you foresee for the dual-career family as it becomes more popular?
Yes, I see life becoming more and more complicated for people rather than simpler, because there are higher expectation levels, people are better educated, and their wants are greater than ever before.
For young and middle-aged couples, one of my major concerns is that they are moving so rapidly that they pay little attention to the fundamental qualities that have always been necessary, regardless of technological advances. The qualities I refer to are personal authenticity, concerns for one another, trust and the need for intimacy. These values are being challenged by transience, impermanence

and interchangeability, leading in some lives to profound feelings of alienation.

Only by allowing ourselves the time to think and to act courageously on what we feel appropriate will we be able to juggle the complexities of personal, family and corporate life.

CHAUVINISM: AT WORK AND AT HOME [6]

The Business Chauvinist

I once had a friend who worked in a largish business corporation in New York City. About four years ago we had lunch together and he was, I thought, in a state of exasperation unlike his normally placid self. "I can't get any useful work done," he complained, "the whole office is like a madhouse, half my colleagues are behaving like madmen. And remind me, I have to buy copies of *Vogue, Glamour* and *Harper's Bazaar* on my way back." This unusual request intrigued me, and I asked the cause of this sudden interest in fashion.

It's like this [he said]. We're concerned about pants suits. Some of the girls have been coming to work in pants suits, and when the management noticed they passed the word down: No pants suits. Well, my secretary turned up with a certificate from her doctor saying that she had suffered from rheumatoid arthritis as a child and that her condition required her to keep her legs warm in the winter. So they made an exception for her; she could hardly be asked to change into a dress at the office, so we had one girl wearing a pants suit. Up until then it had been a fad, something the young women, the secretaries, were pushing for the hell of it—you know, just to annoy the old arteriosclerotic brigade, and they succeeded. . . . We even had memos from the chairman of the board, who hasn't been seen or heard from in ten years! Then all the senior women executives turned up in pants suits, it was like

[6] Excerpts from *Male Chauvinism! How It Works*, by Michael Korda, writer, and editor-in-chief at Simon & Schuster. Random House. '73. p65-7; 162-8. Copyright © 1972, 1973 by Michael Korda. Reprinted by permission of Random House, Inc.

solidarity, and that really scared the pants off the men, if you see what I mean, so we had a meeting in the board room to discuss the problem, and everyone said pants would destroy our image, that some women don't look good in pants, that it was the thin edge of the wedge. Still, when our assistant treasurer, a pretty formidable woman in her fifties, had turned up in pants, there didn't seem much that anyone could do about it. So we decided pants *suits* were OK, provided they were really suits. No slacks, jeans or separate pants. I said, Who the hell knows the difference, but I should have kept my mouth shut, because now we have a committee, the three senior male executives, and we're supposed to decide whether it's a pants suit or just pants. So I have to buy fashion magazines.

The spectacle of three middle-aged men sitting in judgment on the women in their office—like the judgment of Paris by committee—was undeniably comic, and even my friend could see the humor of it. A few months later, I visited his office to find that half the younger women were in pants or blue jeans, a clear failure of policy. "Well," he said, "it's because it's a rainy day. . . . On a rainy, slushy day, it makes sense." By the end of the year, his office looked like a women's college on a weekday morning, and the rapid progression toward total freedom—hot pants, granny dresses, boots, paisleyed gear and braless T-shirts had begun—obliterating all standards, and leaving the men to stagger after it, discarding their ties for turtlenecks and exchanging their Brooks Brothers shoes for a fantastic variety of varnished footwear hitherto seen only on the feet of pimps. . . .

The Domestic Chauvinist

Behind the male chauvinist's supercilious and patronizing attitude toward "all the little girls getting together" lies real fear, the fear that we may no longer be able to impose upon women our vision of ourselves as men. Most men do not control their wives, cannot, possibly don't even want to. Oh yes, they exert as a rule a kind of spurious financial control, but despite the arguments of the radical feminists woman's domestic role gives her far more opportunities for exerting control over domestic decisions than a man, and while it is certainly true that it is the man who goes out and earns the money in the average American marriage, it is notorious that women play the decisive role in determining how that money will be spent. What men want in marriage is not power so much as "face," in the Oriental sense. A woman may dominate a man in any number of ways, provided she allows him to play the dominant role in public, and the surest way for a man to lose prestige among his peers still remains losing an argument with his wife in public.

The price of male chauvinism is terrible confusion; the male chauvinist is trying to combine in one person so many contradictory attitudes toward women that he can only end by fearing and hating them. A powerful and successful speculator I know is a good example of these contradictions. When he appears in public with his wife, he makes it quite clear that he is the boss, and in private conversations he emphasizes that his is an "old-fashioned" marriage. "I make the money, and I don't put up with any nonsense. Somebody has to make decisions, and it's my job to make them." One visit to his home is enough to convince any observer that this is a façade; it is quite obvious that he treads cautiously, stumbling around his house as if he didn't really live there, as if everything in it, furniture, pictures, kitchen appliances, children even, were extensions of his wife's personality, to be treated with extreme care and delicacy. Though inclined to make fun of his wife when he's with other men ("She can't balance a checkbook to save her life, all she needs to make her happy is a charge account, she's terrific with children, but you know, women are a lot more *like* children than men are, they understand them better, they have more patience"), he can switch instantly to her defense, and even use her as his reason for doing something ("If I told my wife I'd said yes to a deal like this she'd laugh her head off, she'd say, What kind of a man are you anyway?"). He grimaces and winks at his young secretary while speaking to his wife on the telephone (I'm not taking any of this seriously, he is implying, it's just my wife talking, gab, gab, gab, that's the way wives are), then sends her out into the streets on a hot July afternoon to pick up theater tickets for the very same woman he's just been making fun of. A man I know has a wife who paints; he makes ritual fun of her efforts when he's with his friends and colleagues (for no man is supposed to take a woman's occupations seriously), but when she has an exhibition, he dragoons every passing acquaintance into going to the exhibit, and stands by the same paintings he has made fun of, saying, "Aren't they great? Isn't she great?"

What is wrong with us that we are willing to settle for such a mass of contradictory attitudes in the one area of life where we should expect consistency? And how can man be expected to have a consistent attitude toward woman— her needs, her role, her ambitions—when their feelings about women are both inconsistent and self-serving? Most men do not see women as fellow human beings at all; they merely have a set of responses toward the idea of women in various roles, from which they can pick and choose the one that seems most appropriate in any given circumstance: domination, submission, sexual passion, patience, fatherly advice, fear, contempt, sentimental adulation. The same man can, within twenty-four hours, shout at his secretary, make a show of negotiating a contract with a woman lawyer on equal terms, make fun of the same women to his colleagues, appear at a party with his wife on his arm, looking strong and protective, and return home listening to her criticize him for behaving like an idiot at the party. Since all these responses, attitudes and postures are constantly getting crossed—fatherly interest serving as a cover-up for lust, a public attitude of domination concealing a private posture of submission, rage at one's secretary compensating for surrender to one's wife—men are inclined to live in a morass of conflicting impulses when it comes to women, however clear-minded they may be about politics, business or technology. "Women," wrote Virginia Woolf, "have served all these centuries as looking glasses possessing the power of reflecting the figure of man at twice its natural size." Yes, men use women as mirrors, but the worst of this is not just that it has reduced women to "looking glasses," it has reduced men to creatures who can only define themselves by means of women. And unfortunately for men the mirror is like the ones in an amusement park that distort and split up the image, showing us to ourselves as a giant with a dwarf's head, or as a pygmy with a gorilla's torso.

Marriage at least serves one purpose: it gives men the chance to come to terms with at least *one* woman. In marriage a man senses the possibility of reducing an infinite problem to finite proportions, of isolating at least one member of this capricious and mysterious species in the hope that this controlled laboratory experiment will either answer his questions or provide a good reason for not asking them. Yet, obstinately, women remain as unfathomable as they were for Sigmund Freud ("The great question that has never been answered, and which I have not yet been able to answer despite my thirty years of research into the feminine soul, is: What does a woman want?"). Isolate a woman, reduce her contacts with the outside world, sleep with her on an exclusive basis, share in the business of living, of procreating, and perhaps we will discover what it is that woman wants, more to the point what she *is*. But no answers are forthcoming so long as we continue to assume that she is radically different and mysterious, so long as we cling to the notion that her biology makes her mind, her "soul" (to use Freud's somewhat ambiguous word) somehow different from our own. If it is different, after all, it must either be inferior or superior, and a large part of what passes for social custom and business convention in our world is in fact a defense set up to convince man that it is he who is superior and she who is limited. The notion that "her" limits are our own is seldom considered. And if we can't find the answer to Sigmund Freud's question, we can always take refuge in the question itself, in the notion that women are after all possessed of some separate sensibility, that there isn't any possibility of "understanding" them in the first place, that by definition they represent a kind of monstrous puzzle that God has created for men to wrestle with hopelessly. We can even be proud of *not* understanding them, for the failure to understand women is the ultimate proof of our masculinity. It is not surprising that Ira Levin, the author of *Rosemary's Baby*, should have chosen as his new horror story the theme of male chauvinism, rightly perceiving that it is a form of modern witchcraft and superstition. In *The Stepford Wives,* Levin shows us a suburban community that seems emptily familiar and unexceptional. A young couple moves there; she is a talented photographer, mildly "liberated," he is a quiet, "reasonable" man. She soon finds that the women around her are remarkably submissive, addicted to housework, unwilling to express an opinion about anything. When Joanna invites her next-door neighbor, Carol, over for a cup of coffee, she refuses, saying, "Thanks, I'd like to, but I have to wax the family room tonight . . . I've put it off too long as it is. It's all over scuff marks . . . There's always something or other that has to be done. You know how it is. I have to finish the kitchen now."

Gradually, Joanna thinks she has discovered that the men of the community have perfected a way of turning their wives into robots, that there is a conspiracy to make each woman into a perfect replica of the male chauvinist husband's ideal. As Joanna says, complimenting the owner of the local drugstore, "You have a lovely wife. Pretty, helpful, submissive to her lord and master; you're a lucky man." "I know," he replies.

In the end Joanna comes to realize that her husband is part of the conspiracy, that whatever is being done is going to be done to her too, and though she fights it, she is caught. When a friend asks her, in the supermarket, how her work is coming along, Joanna replies, "I don't do much photography any more . . . I wasn't especially talented, and I was wasting a lot of time I really have better uses for . . . Housework's enough for me. I used to feel I had to have other interests, but I'm more at ease with myself now. I'm much happier too, and so is my family. That's what counts, isn't it?" She has been turned into a robot too.

There is more significance in this than would at first appear, for both Ira Levin's successes represent a kind of horror-myth portrayal of male chauvinism. In *Rosemary's Baby,* a husband sells his wife to the Devil to further his career as an actor, in *The Stepford Wives,* the ultimate fantasy of male chauvinism is enacted, the recognition that the domestic world men created to enclose women is so important to them as a symbol of power that it need no longer be shared or enjoyed—it is sufficient that it continue to exist!

As a psychoanalyst told me,

I have to spend hours breaking through my [male] patients' defenses. They tell me about their jobs, their houses, the money they make, everything they've done for their families. I have to tell them, "Look, I'm not interested in any of this, I don't care how much your house cost, or about the trip to Europe you took your wife on, you wouldn't be here if you hadn't discovered that your wife doesn't give a damn about any of that, and you have to learn that you don't give a damn either. I don't care how important you are, to me you're a man whose wife thinks he's no good in bed, and it's no good clinging to the $150,000 house as if that were the answer to everything, because if you don't learn to treat her as a person, she will walk out that $150,000 front door, get in her Mercury Cougar convertible, and go off to someone who's alive." The first step in analysis, for me, is teaching men humility, making them understand that it doesn't matter how well they function as businessmen, they have to function as bodies, as people, as lovers. Success in one area doesn't compensate for deficiency in another. I've seen successful men, with male chauvinist attitudes, sit here and weep because their wives are threatening to leave, and most of them say *How could she do this to me?* Well, she did it to him because he isn't a *person* any more, because he's afraid of feeling, living. All he wants is security. And when women begin to think about themselves, the first thing they realize is what we all know: in an existential world there isn't any

security, and there isn't any way a woman can provide security
for someone else. As one woman said to me, "I can't be a liberated
woman and his mother and purpose in life at the same time. I
refuse to be a living proof that *his* life makes sense. Maybe nobody's does."

Men cling to their hope that somebody else will make
sense of their lives, trusting in Theodor Reik's dictum that
"Women in general want to be loved for what they are
and men for what they accomplish." Accomplish enough
and we will be loved, hence the propensity of the domestic male chauvinist to accomplish a great deal, to pour
into his work a disproportionate amount of psychic energy.
Anything is better than admitting that life is a question of
feeling, that nobody can guarantee us anything, that we
cannot demand of another human being that she cut herself off from life to prove to us that we have the capacity,
like small gods, to impose order and security in one small
corner of the universe.

WOMEN IN THE CLERGY [7]

Reprinted from *U.S. News & World Report.*

A new phase now is beginning in the long and uphill
struggle of American women for full acceptance in the
nation's pulpits.

One of the few remaining barriers to women in the
clergy fell on September 16, when the influential Episcopal Church voted to permit ordination of women as priests
and bishops starting January 1 [1977] . . . .

Women's-rights leaders see the vote at the church's
convention in Minneapolis as a landmark advance, cul-
minating years of bitter controversy.

It leaves Roman Catholics, Mormons, Eastern Orthodox members and the most conservative wings of Luther-
anism and Judaism as major holdouts for absolute male
supremacy in the pulpit.

[7] Article in *U.S. News & World Report.* 81:8. S. 27, '76.

Pressure to let women into the clergy now is expected to shift to the nation's 49 million Catholics, who share with 3 million Episcopalians a tradition of male priesthood going back to the Apostles.

Most other denominations have some women ministers, from a handful among the 12 million Southern Baptists to more than 500 in the United Methodist Church. Altogether about 7,000 of the nation's 474,000 clergy are women.

In the last decade, the ratio of women in major Protestant seminaries has jumped from 3 to 16 percent.

As their ranks swell, however, many ordained women find themselves unemployed or stuck in traditional posts as deacons or Sunday-school directors.

Congregations Slow to Accept Women as Pastors

Congregations, they say, are slow to accept women in pastoral roles, such as preaching or officiating at weddings and communion. Moreover, pastorates have fewer openings as membership declines in many of the liberal denominations that encourage female clergy.

The more than 400 women eligible or studying for the Episcopal priesthood will have to compete with a surplus of 1,000 men vying to become priests. The same holds true for the 15 women who brought the issue to a head by receiving irregular ordinations in Philadelphia and Washington over the last two years—unless they win special validation from the convention before it disbands.

Despite earlier threats of schism, most opponents of female ordination are promising to stay—but to fight the spread of women priests at local levels.

Strong resistance was shown in the balloting, with 40 percent or more voting against the change in the House of Bishops and in the House of Deputies, made up of lay and clerical leaders.

Bishops, along with members of local boards, have the authority to select candidates for ordination and pulpits in their own jurisdictions.

Bishop Stanley Atkins of Eau Claire, Wisconsin, warned, however: "I've worked with many women ministers from other denominations, and I've never met one who was pastor of a major congregation. A lot of people will say 'Yes' to women's ordination, but 'No' to a woman as rector of their own church."

Still, some advocates expressed hope that the Episcopal verdict will encourage women's-rights leaders in other denominations—especially in the Roman Catholic Church.

Vatican's Position

Some 1,200 nuns spurred by the Episcopal controversy have launched a movement to push for female Catholic priests. And the Vatican's Biblical Commission, after scouring the Scriptures, ruled there would be no violation of Christ's original intentions if women were allowed in the priesthood, despite firm rejection of the idea by the seventy-nine-year-old Pope Paul VI.

Sister Joyce Manning, one of many Catholic nuns among the crowd of 4,000 packing the Episcopal convention, told the delegates that their approval would provide "a new model of the priesthood" for women of all faiths.

However, Sister Ann Patrick Ware, an ecumenical activist with the National Council of Churches in New York City, gave a more cautious appraisal of the outlook. "This is a great shot in the arm for sisters seeking priesthood in the Catholic Church. But women have so little say in our hierarchy that I don't expect anything to be done about this issue for a long time."

Catholic supporters, like their Episcopalian counterparts, say the different outlooks women are bringing to the clerical profession are long overdue, in terms of religious benefits, as well as women's rights.

Opponents, on the other hand, see women's liberation as one of many secular forces eroding divinely ordained roles and discipline in the Church.

Still, it is clear that women in US churches have made

a major breakthrough that is likely to lend impetus to their drive on remaining bastions of male supremacy in America's pulpits.

TELEVISION AND THE IMAGE OF THE FATHER [8]

On hot nights last summer [1974] I secretly anticipated the day when Rhoda would release me from the torture of watching reruns of Archie yelling at Edith. But when the TV networks launched a new season, my viewing habits changed very little. Monday nights there's Rhoda, but Saturday nights I still watch Archie Bunker and Mary Tyler Moore; weeknights I often settle under a blanket to watch Marcus Welby or Dr. Gannon. On a bad night I may even stay up for the reruns of Perry Mason, my childhood hero. Something about those programs makes me feel warm and cozy inside. While I felt uneasy about enjoying Archie Bunker, I always told myself that watching the good doctors and lawyers was a harmless if unprofitable diversion. Only lately have I begun to realize that the hours I devote to Marcus Welby are a far more telling sign of internal resistance to feminism than are my belly-laugh responses to "All in the Family."

Archie Bunker

Like me, most people instantly, viscerally sense that Archie Bunker is the epitome of male chauvinism. Similarly, many feminists automatically lash out at the construction workers who shout profanities at them—men who have little power to do them real harm—but are taken in by the genial, calm, generous façade of a John Lindsay, an Archibald Cox or a Bishop Paul Moore—their true enemies.

[8] Article entitled "Marcus Welby or Archie Bunker: Will the Real Chauvinist Pig Stand Up?" by Carol Christ, free-lance writer. *Christian Century.* 92: 260-2+. Mr. 12, '75. Copyright 1975 Christian Century Foundation. Reprinted by permission.

Archie Bunker certainly appears to be the archetypal pig. After all, he has his own special chair in the living room (the largest and most comfortable one), he expects his wife and daughter to wait on him, he utters his bigoted opinions for the edification of whoever will listen, and he insists that his views should be agreed with merely because he is paterfamilias. "I'm the man in this house, ain't I?" he yells. What could be more quintessentially chauvinist?

Robert Young, whose starring role as Jim Anderson on "Father Knows Best" was the archetypal forerunner of today's good doctors and lawyers, hardly appears to be a chauvinist pig. Jim Anderson never had a special chair, he never demanded to be waited on, he was no bigot, and he never yelled at anyone. Everything in his home was a model of gentility. His authority rested solely on the fact that he always knew best. And the thing of it is, he actually did. Whenever Bud, Betty or Kathy acted against his better judgment, they either (story No. 1) failed but were forgiven by their understanding father, or (story No. 2) had their project rescued at the last minute by a quick consultation with Father. The power of the calm, quiet, understanding father who always knows best, the image of the Father God, is the power truly to be feared. He is the real male chauvinist pig, the more dangerous because his power rests not on bluster and demands, but on his victim's internalization of the need for judgment and forgiveness.

Archie Bunker's power pales before that of the father who knows best. Archie rarely knows best, as the rest of his family is well aware. Though Edith almost never challenges his opinions directly, she can usually be heard to say "Oh, Archie!" and even more often observed to be secretly hoping he will not be able to carry out his latest threat. His son-in-law is his constant antagonist, and his own daughter almost always sides with her husband against her father. Though he displays the overt trappings of a male chauvinist, Bunker has almost no real authority, even within his own family.

Marcus Welby

In his most recent incarnation as Marcus Welby, Robert Young has changed only his occupation. The program might well have been titled "Doctor Knows Best," because Marcus Welby always does. At first it appears that only Young's sphere of activity has widened: earlier the source of wisdom and authority for his children, he now functions in the same capacity for his patients. There are other subtle differences, however, which, like the current popularity of the male-bonding genre of movies, indicate a deterioration in the status of women in the newer program.

In "Father Knows Best," Jane Wyatt, as Mrs. Anderson, also usually knew best, even if she wasn't the one called in to resolve the crisis. Moreover, father's wisdom supported not only the growth and development of his son, Bud, but also that of his daughters, Betty and Kathy, who were clearly brighter than, and as independent as, their brother. But Marcus Welby has no wife or children. The all-knowing, all-wise father is able to function without the support and devotion Jim Anderson's wife offered. The divine Mother has been suppressed! The distinguished, handsome, genteel Dr. Welby lives with his hairy-armed, super-masculine young white ethnic colleague, Mike Kiley. Like the divine Son, Kiley appears to have been the product of a virgin birth. Kiley's attachments to women, like those of Dr. Welby, are always peripheral, often tinged with condescension (Doctor knows best), and never threaten the more potent male bond between mentor and protégé.

Interestingly, Dr. Welby's authority does not stem from his superior medical knowledge. He often sends his patients to specialists who know far more about a particular disease than he does. This limitation in no way hinders his image, however; moral superiority and wisdom rather than technical knowledge are his specialty. Since the doctor roles are played by Father and Son, who together have all the wisdom and power, women on the program can appear only as patients. Women need saving, men are the saviors.

As might be expected, the healing that Welby offers is primarily not of the body but of the soul. A typical show features a working mother, perhaps a widow or a divorcee, whose child has not received sufficient attention and mothering. Only when she—or, more likely, her child—has a near fatal accident or almost dies from an unusual disease does she realize (with Welby's prodding) that she must put her child's needs before her own. These stories, however, subtly undercut the movement toward female autonomy and integrity as they indicate that even the seemingly liberated woman needs the good father—if not to help her succeed in her career, then to show her how to be a woman and a mother. Similar stories abound on "Medical Center." There Dr. Gannon, played by Chad Everett—who looks exactly like Mike Kiley, but who lacks the super-WASP mentorship of a Dr. Welby—often strong-arms his patients into becoming the kind of women he wants them to be. Even when treated roughly, they always tearfully acknowledge his wisdom in the end.

Owen Marshall

Tall, distinguished-looking Owen Marshall (Arthur Hill), whose canceled series may be expected to return to the tube in reruns, is another of the good fathers. He even looks a little like Robert Young. He too always knows best—not only about the law but also about the psychological health of his clients and their communities. A widower, he is nurtured by a symbiotic relationship with a son-figure (this time not hairy-armed and ethnic-looking but blond and Ivy League) who, like Welby's Kiley, loves his mentor more than any woman. Marshall also has a beautiful, docile, twelve-year-old blonde daughter who occasionally appears with a problem for Father to solve. Unlike real daughters, she never lets her needs interfere with her father's work, and she never complains about his frequent absences from home on out-of-town trips.

On a typical show the superlawyer not only solves his client's legal problems, but also guides her (or him) to a new outlook on life. Sometimes, however, Marshall is allowed to use his superior wisdom to judge an entire community. Here Marshall is asked to defend a social deviant accused of a crime only because he (or more likely she) has a lifestyle or personal values at odds with those of the community. A lesbian schoolteacher accused of seducing a student, a woman teacher accused of murdering a male student with whom she had been in love, and a newsman jailed for failing to reveal his sources are typical objects of Marshall's defense (though the defendant in this last case is a male, the story focused on a female singer, a former addict whom the newsman was protecting). On these programs, Marshall saves his superior moral sensitivity for the summation of the case, and then proceeds to deliver an eloquent sermon directed at the community that brought criminal charges against a defendant whose only crime was holding personal values the community could not accept. Here Marshall plays mediator and savior to the client, and judge and forgiver to the community.

The All-Knowing Father

When, as is often the case, the client or patient of these good fathers is a woman, the message is as old as the patriarchs and as new as a feminist's secret vice (remember that warm cozy feeling I described?). Forgiveness and redemption are the goods sold by these fathers, and women are the buyers. Women who would never dream of heeding the wishes of a truculent, overbearing Bunker type often sell their souls without even realizing it in order to gain the approval of the good father. Even though this approval can be purchased only at the price of admitting one's own inferior moral sensitivity, accepting judgment (guilt), and allowing oneself to be redeemed (guided onto the right path) by internalizing the values of the judge, all too many of us are willing to pay. The gentle, kind exterior of the good father is seductive, and he promises something everyone secretly desires after a hard confrontation with reality. Since he is always right, he promises that whoever stays with him and accepts his judgment and guidance will also be right. Moreover, his constant judgment and the guilt it arouses feed the fear that without him the world would indeed lose its moral bearing.

Now I know where that warm, cozy feeling is coming from. But for some reason, I still watch the programs. My emotional need for the good father seems to be stronger than my intellectual rejection of him. Oh well, maybe if I can confine him to my TV fantasies he won't impinge on my life. I know the danger he presents to me. Too many women continually search for that good father, the one who has an air of genuine authoritativeness, the one who can pull her out of the chaos of moral ambiguity. All too many of us look for him, if not in our own fathers, then in our teachers, lovers, husbands, bosses and psychiatrists —or, failing all else, in our dreams. Somewhere, we cry out in moments of weakness, there must exist that good father who really does know what is best for me. If only I could find him, then I could trust myself to him, and he would provide me the approval I need to justify my life. Even if she has avoided this trap in most areas of her life, a woman may still tell herself that a few hours spent watching Dr. Welby never hurt anyone.

It should be clear by now that the true liberation of women requires the exorcism of the father who knows best, not the humiliation of Archie Bunker. Mary Tyler Moore, the virgin goddess, is still too dependent on Mr. Grant's approval, but maybe Rhoda will yet lead us out of the wilderness.

EQUAL RIGHTS AMENDMENTS: A THREAT
TO FAMILY LIFE? [9]

Voters of New York and New Jersey November 4 [1975] defeated the addition of the Equal Rights Amendment to their states' constitutions. The ERA was defeated in New York by more than 400,000 votes (1.7 million to 1.3 million) and in New Jersey by 60,000 votes (819,133 to 759,369.) Both state legislatures had ratified the ERA to the federal constitution in 1972.

The amendment states, "Equality of rights under the law shall not be denied or abridged on account of sex." Opponents of the ERA were generally credited with a better organized and a more forceful campaign. They used specific arguments: "A vote for the ERA is a vote against the family," or "a vote for homosexual marriage." Many feared that toilets would be unisex, alimony for women abolished, or women would be drafted if the Equal Rights Amendment were passed.

Pittsburgh Post-Gazette
(Editorial, November 8, 1975)

Equal rights amendments to the New York and New Jersey constitutions went down to defeat in Tuesday's elections even though the two states were among the earliest supporters of a similar federal amendment.

We, too, were early supporters of the federal amendment, designed to reaffirm the equal-protection-of-the-laws clause of the United States Constitution and to emphasize the need for expanding equal opportunities for Americans of both sexes. At least that's what we thought the proposed amendment was all about.

We didn't believe the issue had anything to do with attempting to make women who marry, manage house-

[9] From "N.Y., N.J. Voters Defeat State ERA." *Editorials on File.* 6:1370+. N. 1-15, '75. Reprinted with permission from *Editorials on File.* © 1975 Facts on File, Inc.

holds and raise children somehow feel inferior to career women. We didn't believe that it would degenerate into asinine attempts to bastardize the English language, as if the language were the enemy of women's rights. Or to mock the civilized woman's desire to groom and to dress herself attractively, as if intimidating all women to descend to the lowest common denominator of asexual unkemptness is desirable except for the slovenly. Or to impose sexual hiring quotas, as if sex regardless of merit instead of merit regardless of sex should be the operational meaning of equality of opportunity.

The principle was supposed to be that women who have the requisite talent and ability to do a job should have the opportunity. We didn't believe that a movement to accomplish something so eminently sensible as that would come to be dominated in many cases by a tyrannical sisterhood of antidemocrats who wish to force their life-style on the distaff majority through a process of repeated insults euphemistically excused as "consciousness raising,"

We can't blame voters in New York and New Jersey for falling—if that's what they did—for the anti-amendment forces' line that "a vote for the Equal Rights Amendment is a vote against the family."

After all, the "crazies" who muscled their way to women's rights leadership positions or who claimed to be movement spokesmen have screamed their contempt for the family so often and so obstreperously that even a level-headed person might wonder if a goal of these female authoritarians is indeed to force the sexual integration of public rest rooms.

We'll stick with the belief that originally brought us to support the Equal Rights Amendment: that in a highly advanced industrial society the role of the female is increasingly less restricted by economic necessity and that therefore wider opportunity should be made available.

Accordingly, we'll try to shut our ears to the strident

drivel of those girls of whatever age who aspire to womanhood but who haven't the wit or wisdom to attain it.

We don't need to defend women who choose to be fulltime wives and mothers or who earn their living as productive citizens by working in typing pools or by waiting tables. They're far more secure in their womanhood, we believe, than their "sisterly" detractors.

The majority of Americans will come to support equal rights amendments so long as the purpose is kept simple and sensible: to focus attention on sexual discrimination that wastes talent. We understand that frustrating barriers can produce intemperate reactions. Constructive social change, however, is rarely easy. Excesses among its exponents only makes it more difficult.

Los Angeles Times

New York and New Jersey were among the earliest states to ratify the federal Equal Rights Amendment.

But last week the voters in New York and New Jersey defeated state equal rights amendments. Supporters and opponents of ERA agree that women voters brought about the defeats. The anti-ERA forces announced they would begin to work for repeal of the federal ratification.

Well, the news from the East is disappointing. But it should not be read as the end for the ERA. We regard the news as a challenge.

It is a challenge for the ERA supporters . . . to renew their efforts in the fight for full equality under the law.

That, after all, is what the ERA means. It does not mean, as some opponents suggested in the New York and New Jersey elections, that there will be public unisex toilets.

The opponents of ERA rely on scare and hysteria tactics. The ERA will not destroy the American family or the moral fabric of society or even the separation of the sexes where the right of privacy is involved. It will not, we repeat, mean public unisex toilets.

Clearly, the lesson to be learned from the ERA defeats in New York and New Jersey is that ERA supporters must get the facts out to the people.

The facts will be persuasive.

Presidents from Eisenhower to Ford have supported the ERA. The issue is not partisan. The issue is not male against female. The issue is equality under the law, a concept that is basic and essential in a democratic society.

The most important ERA fact is that unless the amendment becomes law, more than half the nation's population will continue to face hypocritical legal barriers that deny women full participation in American life.

V. HEIGHTENED AWARENESS

EDITOR'S INTRODUCTION

One of the means by which women and men have sought to explore and deepen their sense of individuality has been the technique of consciousness-raising. (The terms *consciousness* and *awareness* in this special context of self-knowledge have come into general use though the ideas they connote have by no means won the acceptance of all.)

Language, which transmits human cultural heritage and plays a basic role in child development, is being examined for an understanding of how attitudes and self-images are instilled and how societal traditions are reinforced—a process that obviously continues throughout life. Analyzing language increases awareness, and, reciprocally, increased awareness results in greater language sensitivity.

The first and second articles of this final section illustrate how language can encourage or discourage sexism. A major problem in this area—dealt with in the excerpt from the book *Words and Women*—is that English is largely male-oriented, especially in the use of masculine pronouns. As the authors demonstrate, this unintentionally promotes sex-role conditioning from the earliest comprehension of language.

The second selection is the much-talked-about set of guidelines published by McGraw-Hill Book Company. Designed to raise writers' and editors' consciousness of stereotypical treatment of both sexes in commonly used English, it can help everyone to be aware of linguistic pitfalls. Included are many specific suggestions on how to avoid sexist assumptions in writing.

Heightened and humane awareness, from a male point of view, is the theme of an excerpt from an article by

Susan Edmiston on the personal philosophy and lifestyle of a well-known actor who is deeply and actively committed to a rich family life as well as to a successful career.

The concluding article argues that all is well, in the main. The author, the noted writer Elizabeth Janeway, discusses recent changes in the world that have brought about a reexamination of traditional sex roles. There would now seem to be, she says, no turning back. Once the present awkward stage is over, everyone will benefit.

WHO IS *MAN?* [1]

"The Ascent of Man," the late Jacob Bronowski's acclaimed BBC television series on the evolution of human culture, opens with a program in which the significance of physical adaptation in early hominids is spun in lyric sequence to that watershed of human self-perception, the cave paintings of the Paleolithic period. The series as a whole is remarkable for its stunning and wide-ranging visuals. In this first program two particularly memorable sequences are used to illustrate musculoskeletal development in the only surviving hominid species: scenes of an adult male athlete running and pole-vaulting and poetically executed dissolve shots of a male baby crawling and raising himself to a standing position. The visualizations provide dramatic support for Dr. Bronowski's superb commentary on our beginnings as "man."

To follow the advice of a Bronowski aphorism—ask an impertinent question and you are on the way to a pertinent answer—why did the creators of the program not show either a female athlete or a female baby? If it occurred to them that including a female would provide a more complete and so more accurate image of the human race, why did they reject the idea? Did they feel, con-

[1] Excerpt from *Words and Women*, by Casey Miller and Kate Swift, free-lance writers, photographers, editors. Anchor Press. '76. p 19-38. Copyright © 1976 by Casey Miller and Kate Swift. Used by permission of Doubleday & Company, Inc.

sciously or otherwise, that artistic harmony would somehow be compromised if the descriptions of "man" were matched with pictures of a person clearly not a man? They could scarcely have intended to convey the message that males alone participated in the evolution of humankind, yet through the use of imagery limited to males they effectively negated an inclusive, generic interpretation of their title subject.

In choosing the male to represent the norm, Bronowski and his colleagues were following a long-standing tradition in science. What is remarkable is that the habit persists in the 1970s. Twenty years ago, before the rise of black consciousness in the United States, museum exhibits and textbooks on human evolution often showed a series of male figures or faces on an ascending scale with a Caucasian at the top, a Negro one step below. The racist misinformation such graphs conveyed is exceeded in its arrogance only by the total exclusion of women from the human race.

The failure of the BBC epic either to conceive or to convey a generic interpretation of *man* in that opening program was confirmed by two additional circumstances. One was the treatment of a particularly important fossil skull as an anomaly: it was identified several times as "the skull of an adult female," although other skulls shown were not identified in terms of sex (the subject under discussion was man, of course). The second and stronger evidence emerged in an interview at the end of the hour-long program when, after a climax marked by homage to the cave painters, the host of the series chatted for a few minutes with a guest anthropologist about what women were doing during this early period in the ascent of man.

The use of *man* to include both women and men may be grammatically "correct," but it is constantly in conflict with the more common use of *man* as distinguished from *woman*. This ambiguity renders *man* virtually unusable in what was once its generic sense—a sense all-too-accurately illustrated in Tennyson's line, "Woman is the lesser man."

When Dr. Bronowski said that for years he had been fascinated by "the way in which man's ideas express what is essentially human in his nature," it is anybody's guess whether his vision included all the anonymous women of the past whose ideas and contributions to science and the arts are no less real for never having been identified.

The newspaper headline THREE-CENT PILL LAST HOPE OF MAN suggests that the story to follow may be an announcement by zero-population researchers of a major contraceptive breakthrough, but actually the news item under that particular headline concerned the personal plight of a fifty-one-year-old Wichita, Kansas, man whose only chance for survival was an inexpensive drug called guanidine. Examples of such ambiguity are endless, and the confusion they cause increases as women come to be seen less as the second sex and more as beings who are fully and essentially human.

Most dictionaries give two standard definitions of *man*: a human being, a male human being. A high school student, thinking about these two meanings, may well ask the obvious question, "How can the same word include women in one definition and exclude them in another?" At which point the teacher may dredge up the hoary platitude "Man embraces woman"—which gets a laugh but leaves the question unanswered. And the student, perhaps distracted now by continuing snickers, may feel the question is too trivial (and somehow, if she is a girl, too demeaning) to pursue.

In 1972 two sociologists at Drake University, Joseph Schneider and Sally Hacker, decided to test the hypothesis that *man* is generally understood to embrace *woman*. Some three hundred college students were asked to select from magazines and newspapers a variety of pictures that would appropriately illustrate the different chapters of a sociology textbook being prepared for publication. Half the students were assigned chapter headings like "Social Man," "Industrial Man," and "Political Man." The other half were given different but corresponding headings like

"Society," "Industrial Life," and "Political Behavior." Analysis of the pictures selected revealed that in the minds of students of both sexes use of the word *man* evoked, to a statistically significant degree, images of males only—filtering out recognition of women's participation in these major areas of life—whereas the corresponding headings without *man* evoked images of both males and females. In some instances the differences reached magnitudes of 30 to 40 percent. The authors concluded, "This is rather convincing evidence that when you use the word *man* generically, people do tend to think male, and tend not to think female."

The nature of the pictures chosen was interesting in another way, for they demonstrated that *man* calls up largely negative images of power and dominance. The originators of the research project describe the data gathered at their own university (the largest of three samples studied) as follows:

When we said "Urban Man," as opposed to "Urban Life," students tended to give us pictures portraying sophisticated, upper-middle-class white males and their artifacts—stereos, cars, bachelor apartments, and so on. We also got pictures of disorganization, slums, demolition. The title "Urban Life" also stimulated pictures of ghettos, but in addition there existed a minor theme of hope—people in the park, building construction, and the like.

When we said "Industrial Man" students gave us pictures of heavy, fairly clumsy machinery, and men doing heavy, dirty, or greasy work. We also got the industrial workers' boss—the capitalist, or corporate executive (e.g., of Mack Trucks, Inc., standing in front of a line of his products). When we said "Industrial Life," we more often received pictures of inside craft work, or of scientific-technical work—people operating precision optical instruments, oil refineries, etc.—and more pictures of machines without people.

"Economic Man" primarily yielded pictures of disorganization; people at the mercy of the economic system (cartoons of governmental corruption and waste, white collar crime, shots of unemployed workers, small businesses going bankrupt, store window signs indicating rising prices, etc.). A secondary theme was extravagant consumption of the very wealthy, or again, corporate executives, capitalists. The title "Economic Behavior" also stimulated pictures of disorganization and despair, but they tended toward abstract representation of the economic system in trouble, such as graphs, charts, and so on. But "Economic Behavior" appeared to elicit fewer pictures of capitalists than did the term "Economic Man."

"Political Man" was portrayed by pictures of Nixon or other politicians making speeches to mixed audiences. "Political Behavior" was represented by prominent political figures also, but contained a secondary theme of people, including women and minority males, in political protest situations.

"Social Man" was portrayed as a sophisticated white, party-going male (a third to half of the pictures included consumption of alcohol), usually with women around. "Society" involved scenes of disruption and protest, with a subtheme of cooperation among people—kids of various ethnic origins walking in the woods, for example. . . .

When normative white male behavior is portrayed, it is supposed to be cool, sophisticated, powerful, sometimes muscular, almost always exploitive—(getting more than their fair share). A sort of Norman Mailer ideal self is evoked by the use of the word *man*. *Behavior* and *life,* however, seem to evoke more comprehensively human imagery when people are portrayed. As the image of capitalist, playboy, and hard hat are called forth by the word *man,* so it is the other side of the coin called forth by *behavior* or *life*—women, children, minorities, dissent and protest.

These were the responses of young adults who knew, presumably, how dictionaries define *man*. What does the word mean to children, especially the very young? In dictionaries for beginning readers the "human being" definition of *man* is rarely included because it does not relate to anything in a very young child's experience. To a toddler, a man may be someone who comes to repair the dishwasher, who puts gas in the car, or who appears on the television screen. In the Golden Picture Dictionary for Beginning Readers the full entry for the word is: "Man, men —A boy grows up to be a man. Father and Uncle George are both men." A child may infer from this definition that mother and Aunt Jane are not men. Nobody, least of all a young child, learns the meaning of *man* from a dictionary, but this limited definition does fit the child's experience. A word means what it means not because of what dictionaries say about it, but because most speakers of the language use it with a certain meaning in mind and expect others to use it with the same meaning. If Billy, at age three or four, were to see the "Avon lady" coming up the front walk and say to his mother "Here comes a man," she would correct him. If at nursery school he were asked to draw a picture of a man and he drew a figure that appeared to be a woman, he might well be carted off to a psychiatrist.

In primary school, however, children begin to encounter *man* and *men* in contexts that include people like mother and Aunt Jane and the Avon lady. And despite a conflict with the meaning they already know, they are expected at this stage to acquire an understanding of the other, so-called generic meaning of *man*.

Little is known about how or to what extent this transition in understanding takes place, but Alleen Pace Nilsen touched on the subject in a 1973 study she conducted at the University of Iowa. Using a picture-selection technique with one hundred children ranging in grade level from nursery school through the seventh grade, Nilsen found that *man* in the sentences "Man must work in order to eat" and "Around the world man is happy" was interpreted by a majority of children of both sexes to mean male people and not to mean female people. A correlative survey of beginning textbooks on prehistoric people, all having the word *man* (or *men*) in the title, suggests a possible reason for the children's response. Nilsen found that in these books illustrations of males outnumbered illustrations of females by eight to one.

Prehistoric people were also the focus of a more extensive study involving some five hundred junior high school students in Michigan in 1974. Designed by Linda Harrison of Western Michigan University, the study was aimed at finding out how the students interpreted different terms used to refer to early human beings. Approximately equal numbers of boys and girls taking science courses were asked to complete a survey (which would not be graded) by drawing their impressions of early people as they were described in seven statements on human activities at the dawn of civilization—the use of tools, cultivation of plants, use of fire for cooking, pottery making, care of infants, etc. The statements distributed to one group of students were all phrased in terms of *early man, primitive men, mankind,* and *he.* Students in a second group received the same statements rephrased to refer to *early people, primitive humans,* and *they.* For a third group all the statements were worded in terms of *men and women* and *they.* The students were also asked to label each character they depicted in the arts of cultivating plants, using tools, making pottery, and so forth, with a modern first name. The number of female and male characters drawn by the students in each group were then counted according to the names assigned. (Names that might have applied to either sex were not counted.)

In the group receiving the "man," "men," "mankind," and "he" statements, more students of both sexes drew male figures only than female figures only for every statement except one. The exception related to infant care, but even there 49 percent of the boys and 11 percent of the girls drew males only. Students of both sexes who illustrated the "people" and "humans" statements also tended to draw more males than females. Those who were given statements referring to "men and women" included the greatest number of female characters in their drawings, although here, too, more students of both sexes drew males only than females only.

Harrison, who is a geologist, notes that the male dominance of the students' responses is probably a reflection not only of the language used on the survey but of the language in which human evolution is usually discussed.

The students' apparent impressions that females were not
tool users or plant cultivators are not supported by fossil evidence and inferences about our early predecessors drawn from
analogies with hunting and gathering cultures today [she wrote].
It seems likely that females contributed at least an equal share
in the early development of agriculture, weaving, and pottery,
and to the development of tools used in these endeavors—to the
development of what is normally thought of as evidence of
culture.

Whatever may be known of the contributions females
made to early human culture, an effective linguistic barrier
prevents the assimilation of that knowledge in our present
culture. Studies like those conducted by Harrison, Nilsen,
and Schneider and Hacker clearly indicate that *man* in the
sense of male so overshadows *man* in the sense of human
being as to make the latter use inaccurate and misleading
for purposes both of conceptualizing and communicating.

The "generic man" trap, in which "The Ascent of
Man" was also caught, operates through every kind of me-
dium whenever the human species is being talked about.
Writing in [the New York *Times Magazine*] the psychoanalyst Erich Fromm described man's "vital interests" as
"life, food, access to females, etc." One may be saddened
but not surprised at the statement "man is the only pri-
mate that commits rape." Although, as commonly understood, it can apply to only half the human population, it
is nevertheless semantically acceptable. But "man, being
a mammal, breast-feeds his young" is taken as a joke.

Sometimes the ambiguity of *man* is dismissed on the
grounds that two different words are involved and that
they are homonyms, like a *row* of cabbages and a *row* on
the lake. Two words cannot be homonyms, however, if one
includes the other as does *man* in the first definition given
by the most recent Webster's Collegiate Dictionary: "A
human being, *especially* an adult male human." Since the
definers do not explain who their italicized "especially"
omits, one is left to wonder. Women, children, and adolescent males, perhaps? The unabridged Merriam-Webster

Third New International Dictionary is more precise: man is "a member of the human race: a human being . . . now usually used of males except in general or indefinite applications. . . ."

The meaning of a homonym, like *row* or *bow* or *pool*, is usually clear from its context, but the overlapping definitions of *man* often make its meaning anything but clear. Can we be sure, without consulting the board of directors of the General Electric Company, what the slogan "Men helping Man" was supposed to convey? Since GE employs a large number of women, it should be a safe bet that both female and male employees were in the slogan writer's mind. Yet an ad for the company seems to tip the scales in the other direction: "As long as man is on earth, he's likely to cause problems. But the men at General Electric will keep trying to find answers." Maybe the article *the* is the limiting factor, but it is hard to picture any of "the men at General Electric" as female men. Once again the conscious intention to describe man the human being has been subverted by the more persistent image of man the male.

If it were not for its ambiguity, *man* would be the shortest and simplest English word to distinguish humankind from all other animal species. The Latin scientific label *Homo sapiens* is long, foreign, and the *sapiens* part of questionable accuracy. But at least *homo*—like the Hebrew *'adham*—has the clear advantage of including both sexes. Its inclusiveness is demonstrated by the presence in Latin of the words *mas* and *vir*, both of which signify a male person only and distinguish him unequivocally from *femina* or *mulier*, Latin words for woman. Nevertheless, *homo* is sometimes erroneously understood to mean "male person," and semantic confusion runs riot when it is mistakenly thought to occur in *homosexual*, thereby limiting that term to males. (The prefix *homo-*, as in *homosexual*, *homonym*, and *homogeneous*, comes from the Greek *homos* meaning "same," and its similarity to the Latin *homo* is coincidental.)

To get back to humankind, the Greek word is *anthropos*, from which come words like *anthropology* and *philanthropy* as well as *misanthropy*, a blanket dislike of everybody regardless of sex. Like Latin and Hebrew, Greek has separate words for the sexes—*aner* for a male person (its stem form is *andr-*), *gune* (or *gyne*) for a female person. So in English *misandry* is the little-known partner of *misogyny*; but when the two Greek roots come together in *androgyny*, they describe that rare and happy human wholeness that reverses the destructive linguistic polarization of the sexes.

Although they serve many uses in English, the words for humankind borrowed from classical Greek and Latin have not been called on to resolve the ambiguity of *man*. Native English grew out of a Teutonic branch of the Indo-European family of languages that also produced German, Danish, Norwegian, and Swedish. In the ancestor of all these tongues the word *man* meant a human being irrespective of sex or age. That sense survives in the modern derivitives *mensch* in German, *menneske* in Danish and Norwegian, and *människa* in Swedish, all of which can refer to a woman or a man, a girl or a boy.

The language we speak has no counterpart for these words. However, when *man* was first used in English—as *mann* or sometimes *monn*—it too had the prevailing sense of a human being irrespective of sex and age. About the year 1000 the Anglo-Saxon scholar Aelfric wrote, "His mother was a Christian, named Elen, a very full-of-faith man, and extremely pious." The Oxford English Dictionary cites numerous other examples, including a description written in 1325 of a husband and wife as "right rich men" and a statement from a sermon of 1597 that "The Lord had but one pair of men in Paradise."

At one time English also had separate and unambiguous

words to distinguish a person by sex; *wif* for a female, *wer* and *carl* for a male. *Mann*—a human being—dropped the second *n* in combined forms like *waepman* and *carlman*, both of which meant an adult male person, and *wifman*, an adult female person. *Wifman* eventually became *woman* (the plural, *women*, retains the original vowel sound in the pronunciation of the first syllable), while *wif* was narrowed in meaning to become *wife*. But *wer* and *waepman*, *carl* and *carlman* simply became obsolete; they were no longer needed once *man* was used to signify a male—especially. One cannot help but wonder what would have happened to the word that originally meant a human being if females rather than males had dominated the society in which English evolved through its first thousand years. Would *man* still mean a human being, but especially an adult female?

The question underlines the essential absurdity of using the same linguistic symbols for the human race in one breath and for only half of it in the next. In *Ms Magazine*, Alma Graham, a lexicographer, draws these contrasts:

> If a woman is swept off a ship into the water, the cry is "Man overboard!" If she is killed by a hit-and-run driver, the charge is "manslaughter." If she is injured on the job, the coverage is "workmen's compensation." But if she arrives at a threshold marked "Men Only," she knows the admonition is not intended to bar animals or plants or inanimate objects. It is meant for her.

Alleen Pace Nilsen notes that adults transfer to children their own lack of agreement about when the many compound words like *workman* and *salesman* apply to both sexes and when such compounds are to be used of males only. She offers some examples to illustrate the different levels of acceptability we sense in such words: "My mother's a salesman for Encyclopaedia Britannica" and "Susy wants to be chairman of the dance" are acceptable to many people, but not to all, as is evident from the existence of the terms *saleswoman*, *chairwoman*, and *chairperson*. "Carol Burnett did a one-man show last night" and "Patsy is quite a horseman, isn't she?" are also acceptable, but they draw attention to the discrepancy between the masculine gender term and the subject's sex. "Miss Jones is our mailman" and "Stella Starbuck is KWWL's new weatherman" seem questionable, perhaps because of the newness in relation to women of the activities they describe. "My brother married a spaceman who works for NASA" and "That newsman is in her seventh month of pregnancy" are generally unacceptable.

If adults cannot agree on when a compound of *man* may be a woman, these terms must be doubly confusing to young children, whose understanding of words is limited by their immediate experience. The meaning a child assigns to a word may be quite different from the meaning an adult assumes the child understands. One youngster, for example, when asked to illustrate the incident in the Garden of Eden story where God drives Adam and Eve from the garden, produced a picture of God at the wheel of a pickup truck, with Adam and Eve sitting in the back surrounded by an assortment of flowering plants for their new home. And there is the story of the children who were disappointed to discover that the "dog doctor" was not a dog at all, but an ordinary human being.

It is not really known at what point children begin to come to terms with the dual role the word *man* has acquired or with the generalized use of *he* to mean "either he or she." Certainly the experience is different for boys and girls—ego-enhancing for the former and ego-deflating for the latter. The four-year-old girl who hides her father's pipe and waits for a cue line from him to go find it is *not* expecting to hear "If somebody will find my pipe, I'll give him a big hug." Yet the same child will sooner or later be taught that in such a sentence *him* can also mean *her*.

At a meeting of the Modern Language Association the story was told of twin girls who came home from school in tears one day because the teacher had explained the grammatical rule mandating the use of *he* when the referent is

indefinite or unknown. What emotions had reduced them
to tears? Anger? Humiliation? A sense of injustice? It is unlikely that any woman can recapture her feelings when the
arbitrariness of that rule first struck her consciousness: it
happened a long time ago, no doubt, and it was only one
among many assignments to secondary status.

In reporting on her work with children, Nilsen provides some insights on the different routes boys and girls
travel in accepting the generic use of *he:*

> It is reasonable to conjecture that because of the egocentricity
> which psychologists describe as a normal developmental stage of
> all young children, a boy who is accustomed to hearing such
> words as *he, him,* and *his* used in relationship to himself will feel
> a closer affinity to these terms than will a young girl who has in-
> stead developed an emotional response to *she, her,* and *hers.* . . .
>
> A young boy who is accustomed to hearing himself and his
> possessions . . . referred to with masculine pronouns has excel-
> lent readiness for acquiring the standard formal rules guiding
> the treatment of gender in English. As he expands his world to
> include progressively larger circles of environment and acquaint-
> ances he simply expands the size of the body of things referred
> to with masculine pronouns. It's a very natural process for him to
> learn that every animate being not obviously female is treated as
> masculine. . . . The only unusual requirement is that at some
> stage in his development he learns to include females in the body
> of referents.

For a boy, internalizing the generic interpretation of
masculine pronouns is part of a continuum. He becomes
aware that a symbol which applies to him is reflected
throughout the animate world; a link is strengthened between his own sense of being and all other living things. For
a young girl, no such continuum exists.

> When she begins to expand her environment, unlike the boy,
> she does not simply enlarge her set of referents for the pronouns
> she is already accustomed to. Instead she has to do a reverse
> switch.

If a girl is not to experience a recurring violation of
reality, she must look upon a familiar symbol for herself as
something different and apart from the symbol used for

animate beings in general. Older children are taught that we use *he* as a grammatical convention. In itself that is a slight to girls, but at least it is one they can come to grips with intellectually. Younger children have no way of knowing that the mouse or the turtle or the crocodile referred to as *he* is not necessarily male. "Here he comes," says the TV personality of the woolly bear caterpillar as it marches across the screen. "The groundhog won't see his shadow today," the weather forecaster begins. A national brand of oatmeal has an animal illustration and an "educational" note on each individually packaged serving: "White Tailed Deer. A native of North America, he was the main source of food for early American settlers." "Buffalo. This North American animal roamed the plains in large numbers. He furnished the Indians with food and warm clothing." "Leopard. A member of the cat family, he lives in Africa and Asia. He is a clever hunter." Only ladybugs, cows, hens, and mother animals with their young are predictably called *she*.

The linguistic presumption of maleness is reinforced by the large number of male characters, whether they are human beings or humanized animals, in children's schoolbooks, storybooks, television programs, and comic strips. From Kukla and Ollie to the Cookie Monster, prestigious puppets and fantasized figures all speak with a male voice. And in Scotland, hunters of the Loch Ness monster recently tried to lure "him" with an artificial female monster. In short, the male is the norm, and the assumption that all creatures are male unless they are known to be female is a natural one for children to make.

Some writers and speakers who recognize the generic masculine pronoun as a perpetuator of the male-is-norm viewpoint have begun to avoid using it. [In *Redbook*] Dr. Benjamin Spock, for example, says,

Like everyone else writing in the child-care field, I have always referred to the baby and child with the pronouns *he* and *him*. There is a grammatical excuse, since these pronouns can be used correctly to refer to a girl or woman . . . just as the word *man* may cover women too in certain contexts. But I now agree with the liberators of women that this is not enough of an excuse. The fact remains that this use of the male pronoun is one of many examples of discrimination, each of which may seem of small consequence in itself but which, when added up, help to keep women at an enormous disadvantage—in employment, in the courts, in the universities, and in conventional social life.

A prominent child psychologist, Dr. Lee Salk, comments in the preface to his recent book for parents [*Preparing for Parenthood*]:

> An author interested in eliminating sexism from his or her work is immediately confronted with the masculine tradition of the English language. I personally reject the practice of using masculine pronouns to refer to human beings. Accordingly I have freely alternated my references, sometimes using the female gender and sometimes using the male gender.

If pediatricians and child psychologists tend to be especially sensitive to the harm done by exclusionary language, some linguists are sensitive to what they see as a dangerous precedent when the conventional generic use is replaced by wording like Dr. Salk's "his or her work." James D. McCawley, professor of linguistics at the University of Chicago, maintains that the phrase *he or she* is actually more sexist than *he* alone, which, he says "loses its supposed sexual bias if it is used consistently." In other words, never, never, never qualify the generic pronoun and you will always be understood to include both sexes. "Why not give him or her a subscription to *XYZ* magazine?" asks a promotional letter. A sexist way to word the question, one imagines Professor McCawley advising the advertising agency:

> *He or she* does as much to combat sexism as a sign saying "Negroes admitted" would do to combat racism—it makes women a special category of beings that are left out of the picture unless extra words are added to bring them in explicitly.

McCawley's analogy would be relevant if the sign in question were posted by an organization calling itself "The

White People." But nobody ever uses *white* to mean both white and black, the way *he* is sometimes used to mean both he and she. Alma Graham makes the problem clear by stating it [in *The Columbia Forum*] as a mathematical proposition:

If you have a group half of whose members are A's and half of whose members are B's and if you call the group C, then A's and B's may be equal members of group C. But if you call the group A, there is no way that B's can be equal to A's within it. The A's will always be the rule and the B's will always be the exception—the subgroup, the subspecies, the outsiders.

Admittedly "he or she" is clumsy, and the reasonable argument that it should be alternated with "she or he" makes it still clumsier. Also, by the time any consideration of the pronoun problem gets to this stage, there is usually a large body of opinion to the effect that the whole issue is trivial. Observing that men more often take this view than women, the syndicated columnist Gena Corea has come up with a possible solution. All right, she suggests,

If women think it's important and men don't . . . let's use a pronoun that pleases women. Men don't care what it is as long as it's not clumsy so, from now on, let's use *she* to refer to the standard human being. The word *she* includes *he* so that would be fair. Anyway, we've used *he* for the past several thousand years and we'll use *she* for the next few thousand; we're just taking turns.

Men who work in fields where women have traditionally predominated—as nurses, secretaries, and primary school teachers, for example—know exactly how Corea's proposed generic pronoun would affect them: they've tried it and they don't like it. Until a few years ago most publications, writers, and speakers on the subject of primary and secondary education used *she* in referring to teachers. As the proportion of men in the profession increased, so did their annoyance with the generic use of feminine pronouns. By the mid-1960s, according to the journal of the National Education Association, some of the angry young men in

teaching were claiming that references to the teacher as
"she" were responsible in part for their poor public image
and, consequently, in part for their low salaries. One man,
speaking on the floor of the National Education Association
Representative Assembly, said,

> The incorrect and improper use of the English language is a
> vestige of the nineteenth century image of the teacher, and con-
> flicts sharply with the vital image we attempt to set forth today.
> The interests of neither the women nor of the men in our pro-
> fession are served by grammatical usage which conjures up an
> anachronistic image of the nineteenth century schoolmarm."

Here is the male-is-norm argument in a nutshell. Although the custom of referring to elementary and secondary
school teachers as "she" arose because most of them were
women, it becomes grammatically "incorrect and improper"
as soon as men enter the field in more than token numbers.
Because the use of *she* excludes men, it conflicts with the
"vital image" teachers attempt to project today. Women
teachers are still in the majority, but the speaker feels it is
neither incorrect nor improper to exclude them linguis-
tically. In fact, he argues, it is proper to do so because the
image called up by the pronoun *she* is that of a schoolmarm.
To be vital, it appears, a teacher's image must be male.

No "schoolmarm" was responsible for making *man* and
he the subsuming terms they have become, though female
schoolteachers—to their own disadvantage—dutifully taught
the usages schoolmasters decreed to be correct. Theodore
M. Bernstein and Peter Farb, contemporary arbiters of
usage, also invoke "schoolmarms" when they want to blame
someone for what they consider overconservatism. Bernstein calls his scapegoat "Miss Thistlebottom" and Farb
calls his "Miss Fidith." But on the matter of generic singular pronouns, both men defend the rule that says *he* is the
only choice. Ethel Strainchamps, who eschews the role of
arbiter, calls that "a recent Mr. Fuddydud 'rule'" and cites
examples of contrary usage from the *Oxford English Dictionary* to prove her point.

By and large, however, the "correctness" of using *man* and *he* generically is so firmly established that many people, especially those who deal professionally with English, have difficulty recognizing either the exclusionary power of these words or their failure to communicate reality. In fact the yearning to understand masculine terminology as including both sexes is sometimes so strong that it asserts itself in defiance of literary or historic evidence to the contrary. Of *course* Alexander Pope's admonition, "Know then thyself . . . the proper study of mankind is man," was intended to include women, we say. But the reader to whom these lines were addressed is made more specific by the author's later reference in the same work to "thy dog, thy bottle, and thy wife."

It was Pope's custom to write his philosophical poems in the form of epistles to particular individuals, and *An Essay on Man,* published in 1733, was written to his friend Henry St. John, Lord Bolingbroke. Today most readers probably infer that the particular is being made general, that the specific man, Bolingbroke, represents generic "man" in the poet's mind. Pope may have thought so too, but that doesn't solve the linguistic problem. In the unlikely event that he had addressed *An Essay on Man* to a woman instead of to a man, would he have made a categorical reference to her dog, her bottle, and her husband? The question is not as frivolous as it sounds, for the issue is essentially one of categories and what they are understood to include or omit. Women—and in this case wives—are understood to be a category included in generic man. When women are separated from man and grouped with other non-man items like dogs and bottles, the effect on generic man is scarcely noticeable: the subject of the "proper study" remains intact. But if men—and, by extension, husbands—were to be considered a discrete category and were separated from the whole, what would happen to generic man? Would "he" be allowed to consist entirely of women, as he is often allowed to consist entirely of men?

In the spring of 1776, when John Adams and his colleagues in Congress were preparing to dissolve the political bands that connected the thirteen colonies to Great Britain, Abigail Adams wrote to her husband:

In the new code of laws which I suppose it will be necessary for you to make, I desire you would remember the ladies and be more generous and favorable to them than your ancestors. Do not put such unlimited power in the hands of the husbands. Remember, all men would be tyrants if they could. If particular care and attention is not paid to the ladies, we are determined to foment a rebellion, and will not hold ourselves bound by any laws in which we have no voice or representation.

Abigail Adams was plainly excluding women from her phrase *all men would be tyrants* for she went on to say:

That your sex are naturally tyrannical is a truth so thoroughly established as to admit of no dispute; but such of you as wish to be happy willingly give up the harsh title of master for the more tender and endearing one of friend.

To which John Adams replied:

As to your extraordinary code of laws, I cannot but laugh. We have been told that our struggle has loosened the bonds of government everywhere; that children and apprentices were disobedient; that schools and colleges were grown turbulent; that Indians slighted their guardians, and Negroes grew insolent to their masters. But your letter was the first intimation that another tribe, more numerous and powerful than all the rest, were grown discontented.

When the Declaration of Independence was issued in Philadelphia a few months later, the self-evident truths that "all men are created equal" and that "governments are instituted among men, deriving their just powers from the consent of the governed," did not apply to women any more than they did to men who were slaves or to those original inhabitants of the country referred to in the document as "the merciless Indian savages."

Lessons in American history provide many more examples of how the part played by women has been distorted or omitted through the use of terminology presumed to be generic. School children are taught, for instance, that the early colonists gained valuable experience in self-government. They learn that the Indians, though friendly at first, soon began to plunder the frontier settlements. They are told that pioneers pushed westward, often taking their wives, children, and household goods with them. A child may wonder whether women were involved in the process of self-government or were among the plunderers of frontier settlements, or the child may accept the implication that women were not themselves colonists or Indians or pioneers, but always part of the baggage.

"Man is the highest form of life on earth," the *Britannica Junior Encyclopaedia* explains. "His superior intelligence, combined with certain physical characteristics, have enabled man to achieve things that are impossible for other animals." The response of a male child to this information is likely to be "Wow!"—that of a female child, "Who? Do they mean me too?" Even if the female child understands that yes, she too is part of man, she must still leap the hurdles of all those other terms that she knows from her experience refer to males only. When she is told that we are all brothers, that the brotherhood of man includes sisters, and that the faith of our fathers is also the faith of our mothers, does she really believe it? How does she internalize these concepts? "We must understand that 'the brotherhood of man' does not exclude our beloved sisters," the eminent scholar Jacques Barzun says [in *The Columbia Forum*]. "But how do we accomplish that feat? By an act of will? By writing it on the blackboard a hundred and fifty times? Cases are pending in a dozen courtrooms today questioning this very understanding.

The subtle power of linguistic exclusion does not stop in the schoolroom, and it is not limited to words like *man, men, brothers, sons, fathers,* or *forefathers.* It is constantly being extended to words for anyone who is not female by definition. Musing on the nature of politics, for example, a television commentator says, "People won't give up power. They'll give up anything else first—money, home, wife, children—but not power." A sociologist, discussing the correlates of high status, reports that "Americans of higher status have more years of education, more children attending college, less divorce, lower mortality, better dental care, and less chance of having a fat wife." Members of the women's movement in France were arrested for displaying the slogan "One Frenchman in Two Is a Woman"; it was taken by some outraged French males to mean that 50 percent of their number were homosexuals.

If these items appear to be molehills, it must be remembered that the socializing process, that step-by-step path we follow in adapting to the needs of society, is made up of many small experiences that often go unnoticed. Given the male milieu, it becomes natural to think of women as an auxiliary and subordinate class, and from there is it an easy jump to see them as a minority or a special interest group. A few years ago an authority on constitutional law wrote in *Fortune* magazine:

> Various kinds of claims are working their way through the judicial system, and the Supreme Court may ultimately have to face them—suits seeking judicial determination of abortion statutes, the death penalty, environmental issues, the rights of women, the Vietnam war.

If the Supreme Court is ever asked to make a judicial determination of "the rights of men," it will be a sign that the rights of women and the rights of men have finally become parallel and equal constituents of human rights.

Some authorities, including Professor Barzun, insist that *man* is still a universal term clearly understood to mean *person,* but the mass of evidence is against that view. As early as 1752, when David Hume referred in his *Political Discourses* to "all men, male and female," the word had to be qualified if it was not to be misunderstood. Dr. Richard P. Goldwater, a psychotherapist, goes to the heart of the matter when he asks:

If we take on its merits [the] assertion that *man* in its deepest origin of meaning stands for both sexes of our race, then how did it come to mean *male*? Did we males appropriate *man* for ourselves at the expense of the self-esteem of our sisters? Did what we now call "sexism" alter the flow of language through us?"

Those who have grown up with a language that tells them they are at the same time men and not men are faced with ambivalence—not about their sex, but about their status as human beings. For the question "Who is man?" it seems, is a political one, and the very ambiguity of the word is what makes it a useful tool for those who have a stake in maintaining the status quo.

ELIMINATING BIAS IN PUBLICATIONS [2]

About These Guidelines

The word *sexism* was coined, by analogy to *racism,* to denote discrimination based on gender. In its original sense, *sexism* referred to prejudice against the female sex. In a broader sense, the term now indicates any arbitrary stereotyping of males and females on the basis of their gender.

We are endeavoring through these guidelines to eliminate sexist assumptions from McGraw-Hill Book Company publications and to encourage a greater freedom for all individuals to pursue their interests and realize their potentials. Specifically, these guidelines are designed to make McGraw-Hill staff members and McGraw-Hill authors aware of the ways in which males and females have been stereotyped in publications; to show the role language has played in reinforcing inequality; and to indicate positive approaches toward providing fair, accurate, and balanced treatment of both sexes in our publications.

One approach is to recruit more women as authors and contributors in all fields. The writings and viewpoints of

[2] Pamphlet entitled *Guidelines for Equal Treatment of the Sexes in McGraw-Hill Publications.* McGraw-Hill. ['74]

ould be represented in quotations and references
possible. Anthologies should include a larger
of selections by and about women in fields
able materials are available but women are currently underrepresented.

Women as well as men have been leaders and heroes,
explorers and pioneers, and have made notable contributions to science, medicine, law, business, politics, civics,
economics, literature, the arts, sports, and other areas of
endeavor. Books dealing with subjects like these, as well as
general histories, should acknowledge the achievements of
women. The fact that women's rights, opportunities, and
accomplishments have been limited by the social customs
and conditions of their time should be openly discussed
whenever relevant to the topic at hand.

We realize that the language of literature cannot be prescribed. The recommendations in these guidelines, thus, are
intended primarily for use in teaching materials, reference
works, and nonfiction works in general.

1. The Roles of Women and Men

Men and women should be treated primarily as people,
and not primarily as members of opposite sexes. Their
shared humanity and common attributes should be stressed
—not their gender difference. Neither sex should be stereotyped or arbitrarily assigned to a leading or secondary role.

Avoiding Job Stereotypes. Though many women will
continue to choose traditional occupations such as homemaker or secretary, women should not be type-cast in these
roles but shown in a wide variety of professions and trades:
as doctors and dentists, not always as nurses; as principals
and professors, not always as teachers; as lawyers and
judges, not always as social workers; as bank presidents,
not always as tellers; as members of Congress, not always as
members of the League of Women Voters.

Similarly, men should not be shown as constantly subject to the "masculine mystique" in their interests, attitudes,

or careers. They should not be made to feel that their self-worth depends entirely upon their income level or the status level of their jobs. They should not be conditioned to believe that a man ought to earn more than a woman or that he ought to be the sole support of a family.

An attempt should be made to break job stereotypes for both women and men. No job should be considered sex-typed, and it should never be implied that certain jobs are incompatible with a woman's "femininity" or a man's "masculinity." Thus, women as well as men should be shown as accountants, engineers, pilots, plumbers, bridge-builders, computer operators, TV repairers, and astronauts, while men as well as women should be shown as nurses, grade-school teachers, secretaries, typists, librarians, file clerks, switchboard operators, and baby-sitters.

Women with a profession should be shown at all professional levels, including the top levels. Women should be portrayed in positions of authority over men and over other women, and there should be no implication that a man loses face or that a woman faces difficulty if the employer or supervisor is a woman. All work should be treated as honorable and worthy of respect; no job or job choices should be downgraded. Instead, women and men should be offered more options than were available to them when work was stereotyped by sex.

Life Style. Books designed for children at the preschool, elementary, and secondary levels should show married women who work outside the home and should treat them favorably. Teaching materials should not assume or imply that most women are wives who are also full-time mothers, but should instead emphasize the fact that women have choices about their marital status, just as men do: that some women choose to stay permanently single and some are in no hurry to marry; that some women marry but do not have children, while others marry, have children, and continue to work outside the home. Thus, a text might say that some married people have children and some do not, and that sometimes *one or both parents* work outside the home. Instructional materials should never imply that all women have a "mother instinct" or that the emotional life of a family suffers because a woman works. Instead they might state that when both parents work outside the home there is usually either greater sharing of the child-rearing activities or reliance on day care centers, nursery schools, or other help.

According to Labor Department statistics for 1972, over 42 percent of all mothers with children under eighteen worked outside the home, and about a third of these working mothers had children under six. Publications ought to reflect this reality.

Both men and women should be shown engaged in home maintenance activities, ranging from cooking and housecleaning to washing the car and making household repairs. Sometimes the man should be shown preparing the meals, doing the laundry, or diapering the baby, while the woman builds bookcases or takes out the trash.

Career Options. Girls should be shown as having, and exercising, the same options as boys in their play and career choices. In school materials, girls should be encouraged to show an interest in mathematics, mechanical skills, and active sports, for example, while boys should never be made to feel ashamed of an interest in poetry, art, or music, or an aptitude for cooking, sewing, or child care. Course materials should be addressed to students of both sexes. For example, home economics courses should apply to boys as well as girls, and shop to girls as well as boys. Both males and females should be shown in textbook illustrations depicting career choices.

When as a practical matter it is known that a book will be used primarily by women for the life of the edition (say, the next five years), it is pointless to pretend that the readership is divided equally between males and females. In such cases it may be more beneficial to address the book fully to women and exploit every opportunity (1) to point out to them a broader set of options than they might otherwise have considered, and (2) to encourage them to aspire to a more active, assertive, and policymaking role than they might otherwise have thought of.

Women and girls should be portrayed as active participants in the same proportion as men and boys in stories, examples, problems, illustrations, discussion questions, test items, and exercises, regardless of subject matter. Women should not be stereotyped in examples by being spoken of only in connection with cooking, sewing, shopping, and similar activities.

2. Portrayals: Human Terms

Members of both sexes should be represented as whole human beings with *human* strengths and weaknesses, not masculine or feminine ones. Women and girls should be shown as having the same abilities, interests, and ambitions as men and boys. Characteristics that have been traditionally praised in males—such as boldness, initiative, and assertiveness—should also be praised in females. Characteristics that have been praised in females—such as gentleness, compassion, and sensitivity—should also be praised in males.

Like men and boys, women and girls should be portrayed as independent, active, strong, courageous, competent, decisive, persistent, serious-minded, and successful. They should appear as logical thinkers, problem-solvers, and decision makers. They should be shown as interested in their work, pursuing a variety of career goals, and both deserving of and receiving public recognition for their accomplishments.

Sometimes men should be shown as quiet and passive, or fearful and indecisive, or illogical and immature. Similarly, women should sometimes be shown as tough, aggressive, and insensitive. Stereotypes of the logical, objective male and the emotional, subjective female are to be avoided. In descriptions, the smarter, braver, or more successful person should be a woman or girl as often as a man or boy. In illustrations, the taller, heavier, stronger, or more active person should not always be male, especially when children are portrayed.

Descriptions of Men and Women. Women and men should be treated with the same respect, dignity, and seriousness. Neither should be trivialized or stereotyped, either in text or in illustrations. Women should not be described by physical attributes when men are being described by mental attributes or professional position. Instead, both sexes should be dealt with in the same terms. References to a man's or a woman's appearance, charm, or intuition should be avoided when irrelevant.

NO	YES
Henry Harris is a shrewd lawyer and his wife Ann is a striking brunette.	The Harrises are an attractive couple. Henry is a handsome blond and Ann is a striking brunette.
	or
	The Harrises are highly respected in their fields. Ann is an accomplished musician and Henry is a shrewd lawyer.
	or
	The Harrises are an interesting couple. Henry is a shrewd lawyer and Ann is very active in community (*or* church *or* civic) affairs.

In descriptions of women, a patronizing or girl-watching tone should be avoided, as should sexual innuendoes, jokes, and puns. Examples of practices to be avoided: focusing on physical appearance (a buxom blonde); using special female-gender word forms (poetess, aviatrix, usherette); treating women as sex objects or portraying the typical woman as weak, helpless, or hysterical; making women figures of fun or objects of scorn and treating their issues as humorous or unimportant.

Examples of stereotypes to be avoided: scatterbrained female, fragile flower, goddess on a pedestal, catty gossip, henpecking shrew, apron-wearing mother, frustrated spinster, ladylike little girl. Jokes at women's expense—such as the woman driver or nagging mother-in-law clichés—are to be avoided.

NO	YES
the fair sex; the weaker sex	*women*
the distaff side	*the female side* or *line*
the girls or *the ladies* (when adult females are meant)	*the women*
girl, as in: I'll have my *girl* check that.	I'll have my *secretary* (or my *assistant*) check that. (Or use the person's name.)
lady used as a modifier, as in *lady* lawyer	*lawyer* (A woman may be identified simply through the choice of pronouns, as in: *The lawyer made her summation to the jury.* Try to avoid gender modifiers altogether. When you *must* modify, use *woman* or *female,* as in: *a course on women writers,* or *the airline's first female pilot.*)

NO	YES
the little woman; the better half; the ball and chain	wife
female-gender word forms, such as *authoress, poetess, Jewess*	author, poet, Jew
female-gender or diminutive word forms, such as *suffragette, usherette, aviatrix*	suffragist, usher, aviator (or *pilot*)
libber (a put-down)	feminist; liberationist
sweet young thing	young woman; girl
co-ed (as a noun)	student

(*Note:* Logically, *co-ed* should refer to any student at a co-educational college or university. Since it does not, it is a sexist term.)

NO	YES
housewife	homemaker for a person who works at home, or rephrase with a more precise or more inclusive term
career girl or career woman	name the woman's profession: *attorney Ellen Smith; Marie Sanchez, a journalist* or *editor* or *business executive* or *doctor* or *lawyer* or *agent*
cleaning woman, cleaning lady, or maid	housekeeper; house or office cleaner

NO	*YES*
The sound of the drilling disturbed the housewives in the neighborhood.	The sound of the drilling disturbed everyone within earshot (or everyone in the neighborhood).
Housewives are feeling the pinch of higher prices.	Consumers (customers or shoppers) are feeling the pinch of higher prices.

In descriptions of men, especially men in the home, references to general ineptness should be avoided. Men should not be characterized as dependent on women for meals, or clumsy in household maintenance, or as foolish in self-care.

To be avoided: characterizations that stress men's dependence on women for advice on what to wear and what to eat, inability of men to care for themselves in times of illness, and men as objects of fun (the henpecked husband).

Women should be treated as part of the rule, not as the exception. Generic terms, such as *doctor* and *nurse,* should be assumed to include both men and women, and modified titles such as "woman doctor" or "male nurse" should be avoided. Work should never be stereotyped as "woman's work" or as "a man-sized job." Writers should avoid showing a "gee-whiz" attitude toward women who perform competently. ("Though a woman, she ran the business as well as any man" or "Though a woman, she ran the business efficiently.")

Women as Participants in the Action. Women should be spoken of as participants in the action, not as possessions of the men. Terms such as *pioneer, farmer,* and *settler* should not be used as though they applied only to adult males.

NO	YES
Pioneers moved West, taking their wives and children with them.	Pioneer families moved West.
	Pioneer men and women (*or* pioneer couples) moved West, taking their children with them.

Women should not be portrayed as needing male permission in order to act or to exercise rights (except, of course, for historical or factual accuracy).

NO	YES
Jim Weiss allows his wife to work part time.	Judy Weiss works part time.

Women should be recognized for their own achievements. Intelligent, daring, and innovative women, both in history and in fiction, should be provided as role-models for girls, and leaders in the fight for women's rights should be honored and respected, not mocked or ignored.

3. Language Considerations

In references to humanity at large, language should operate to include women and girls. Terms that tend to exclude females should be avoided whenever possible.

The word *man* has long been used not only to denote a person of male gender, but also generically to denote humanity at large. To many people today, however, the word *man* has become so closely associated with the first meaning (a male human being) that they consider it no longer broad enough to be applied to any person or to human beings as a whole. In deference to this position, alternative expressions should be used in place of *man* (or derivative constructions used generically to signify humanity at large) whenever such substitutions can be made without producing an awkward or artificial construction. In cases where *man*-words must be used, special efforts should be made to ensure that pictures and other devices make explicit that such references include women.

Here are some possible substitutions for *man*-words:

NO	YES
mankind	humanity, human beings, human race, people
primitive man	primitive people or peoples; primitive human beings; primitive men and women
man's achievements	human achievements
If a man drove 50 miles at 60 mph . . .	If a person (or driver) drove 50 miles at 60 mph . . .
the best man for the job	the best person (or candidate) for the job
man-made	artificial; synthetic, manufactured; constructed; of human origin
manpower	human power; human energy; workers; workforce
grow to manhood	grow to adulthood; grow to manhood or womanhood

Pronouns. The English language lacks a generic singular pronoun signifying *he* or *she*, and therefore it has been customary and grammatically sanctioned to use masculine pronouns in expressions such as "one . . . *he*," "anyone . . .

he," and "each child opens *his* book." Nevertheless, avoid
when possible the pronouns *he, him,* and *his* in reference
to the hypothetical person or humanity in general.

Various alternatives may be considered:

(1) Reword to eliminate unnecessary gender pronouns.

NO	*YES*
The average American drinks his coffee black.	The average American drinks black coffee.

(2) Recast into the plural.   Most Americans drink
                               their coffee black.

(3) Replace the masculine pronoun with *one, you, he or
she, her or his,* as appropriate. (Use *he or she* and its vari-
ations sparingly to avoid clumsy prose.)

(4) Alternate male and female expressions and examples.

NO	*YES*
I've often heard supervisors say, "He's not the right man for the job," or "He lacks the qualifications for success."	I've often heard supervisors say, "She's not the right person for the job," or "He lacks the qualifications for success."

(5) To avoid severe problems of repetition or inept wording, it may sometimes be best to use the generic *he* freely,
but to add, in the preface and as often as necessary in the
text, emphatic statements to the effect that the masculine
pronouns are being used for succinctness and are intended
to refer to both females and males.

These guidelines can only suggest a few solutions to
difficult problems of rewording. The proper solution in
any given passage must depend on the context and on the
author's intention. For example, it would be wrong to

pluralize in contexts stressing a one-to-one relationship, as between teacher and child. In such cases, the expression *he or she* or either *he* or *she* as appropriate will be acceptable.

Occupations. Occupational terms ending in *man* should be replaced whenever possible by terms that can include members of either sex unless they refer to a particular person who is in fact male. (Each occupational title suggested below is already in wide use.)

NO	YES
congressman	member of Congress; representative (but Congress-*man* Koch and Congress-*woman* Holtzman)
businessman	business executive; business manager
fireman	fire fighter
mailman	mail carrier; letter carrier
salesman	sales representative; salesperson; sales clerk
insurance man	insurance agent
statesman	leader; public servant
chairman	person presiding at (or chairing) a meeting; presiding officer; the chair; head; leader; coordinator; moderator
cameraman	camera operator
foreman	supervisor

Language that assumes all readers are male should be avoided.

NO	YES
you and your wife	you and your spouse
when you shave in the morning	when you brush your teeth (or wash up) in the morning

4. Parallel Treatment

The language used to designate and describe females and males should treat the sexes equally.

Parallel language shoud be used for women and men.

NO	YES
the men and the ladies	the men and the women the ladies and the gentlemen the girls and the boys
man and wife	husband and wife

Note that *lady* and *gentleman, wife* and *husband,* and *mother* and *father* are role words. *Ladies* should be used for women only when men are being referred to as *gentlemen.* Similarly, women should be called *wives* and *mothers* only when men are referred to as *husbands* and *fathers.* Like a male shopper, a woman in a grocery store should be called a *customer,* not a *housewife.*

Names. Women should be identified by their own names (e.g., Indira Gandhi). They should not be referred to in terms of their roles as wife, mother, sister, or daughter unless it is in these roles that they are significant in context. Nor should they be identified in terms of their marital relationships (Mrs. Gandhi) unless this brief form is stylistically more convenient (than, say Prime Minister Gandhi) or is paired up with similar references to men.

A woman should be referred to by name in the same way that a man is. Both should be called by their full names, by first or last name only, or by title.

NO	YES
Bobby Riggs and Billie Jean	Bobby Riggs and Billie Jean King
Billie Jean and Riggs	Billie Jean and Bobby
Mrs. King and Riggs	King and Riggs Ms. King (because she prefers Ms.) and Mr. Riggs
Mrs. Meir and Moshe Dayan	Golda Meir and Moshe Dayan or Mrs. Meir and Dr. Dayan

Unnecessary reference to or emphasis on a woman's marital status should be avoided. Whether married or not, a woman may be referred to by the name by which she chooses to be known, whether her name is her original name or her married name.

Whenever possible, a term should be used that includes both sexes. Unnecessary references to gender should be avoided.

NO	YES
college boys and co-eds	students

Titles. Insofar as possible, job titles should be nonsexist. Different nomenclature should not be used for the same job depending on whether it is held by a male or by a female. (See under Occupations, above, for additional examples of words ending in *man*.)

NO	YES
steward or purser or stewardess	flight attendant
policeman and policewoman	police officer
maid and houseboy	house or office cleaner; servant

Different pronouns should not be linked with certain work or occupations on the assumption that the worker is always (or usually) female or male. Instead either pluralize or use *he or she* and *she or he*.

NO	YES
the consumer or shopper . . . she	consumers or shoppers . . . they
the secretary . . . she	secretaries . . . they
the breadwinner . . . his earnings	the breadwinner . . . his or her earnings *or* breadwinners . . . their earnings.

Males should not always be first in order of mention. Instead, alternate the order, sometimes using: *women and men, gentlemen and ladies, she or he, her or his.*

A WHOLE HUMAN BEING [3]

In the world of celebrities Alan Alda is something extraordinary—an adult. In magazine and newspaper articles, recent observers have focused on his niceness—his devotion to his family, his courtesy to other human beings, his hu-

[3] From article, "Alan Alda: America's Sweetheart," by Susan Edmiston, free-lance writer. *Redbook.* 147:88+. Jl. '76. Excerpted from *Redbook Magazine* July 1976. Copyright © 1976 by The Redbook Publishing Company.

mane stand on all the right issues. If F. Scott Fitzgerald was correct when he wrote, "A sense of the fundamental decencies is parceled out unequally at birth," Alan Alda got more than his share.

But Alda is something more complicated than just a nice guy. He is that interesting combination, a man ambitious and successful in his professional life who also is intensely concerned about his emotional and personal life. He is perhaps the only male celebrity to whom the question traditionally asked female stars—"If it ever came to a choice, which would you give up, your career or your family?"—would be a meaningful one. (He would never give up either.) You might say that he has the kind of personality that's recently been labeled "androgynous," combining strengths and values traditionally associated with both masculinity and femininity. Or you could just say that he's a whole human being, interested in what Freud said were the two essentials of a truly human life—love and work.

In recent years, work has made Alan Alda a star. In 1974 he won the Emmy for best lead actor in a comedy series as Captain Hawkeye in *M*A*S*H,* and last year shared honors with Telly Savalas in the People's Choice poll as television's favorite male actor. His role in the TV series about a medical unit in the Korean War is meaningful to him; he believes in the humanitarian message of *M*A*S*H* and feels his work in it represents his best acting. At the same time, his work has tested his personal values—his commitment to his wife [Arlene Weiss Alda, a clarinetist and photographer] and children and the life they have built together over the past ten years in a small town in New Jersey.

Rather than live in California ("There's no there there," Alan once said, quoting Gertrude Stein), they decided to stay where they had put down roots and where their three teen-aged daughters, Eve, Elizabeth and Beatrice, lead lives just like those of the children in the community whose parents are less glamorously employed. "The Aldas didn't give up their life-style for Alan's career," says long-time friend Marlo Thomas, "even though his career at the moment is in Hollywood. They tried it out there, but they're committed more to what's good for them as a family than what's good for his work." . . .

"I've always been a feminist . . . [Alda says]. Even as a little kid I was aware that it was silly that women were supposed to grow up to be nurses and men to be doctors."

He'd shared in the care of his children from the very beginning.

I was in a unique position to help [he jokes]. I was out of work a lot. As soon as I had the courage to lift our first kid—which took a couple of months because I was afraid of breaking her—I diapered her and fed her and took her out in the carriage. Those were the days of real diapers, you know. We'd clean them out by flushing them in the toilet bowl, and in the wintertime the toilet water is very cold and we had three kids one after another and for three years I had my hand permanently frozen.

The Equal Rights Amendment currently heads the list of Alan's political priorities.

I get asked to do a lot of things, but it's the *only* thing I'll drop everything for [he says]. When I see a confident, individualistic woman—somebody that's not been trapped by the aura of submissiveness that women have had to assume for centuries —I'm just really moved by it. I love to see a person, against the odds, against the expectation of the culture, exist with a sense of self.

Among Alan's greatest admirers are the feminists he's worked with for the ERA [Equal Rights Amendment]. Marlo Thomas, who campaigned for the amendment with him in Miami, describes him as "a really fair human being —he should be a judge—but on top of it he's got this terrific wit. He doesn't do anything petty or mean, he's not selfish, he doesn't take advantage of the situation, he doesn't think only of himself. You never have to be suspicious of his motives."

Republican Congresswoman Margaret Heckler, of Massachusetts, who until this past April [1976] cochaired with Alan a presidential subcommittee on the Equal Rights Amendment, puts it another way:

He typifies what is best about the Women's Movement and the attitude of the enlightened men who support it. In everything he does there's a great spirit of sharing and generosity. And he's a delight to be with—just a delight. . . .
I think he's sensational and I think he's going to be a very potent force in the movement for equal rights. Unfortunately, there are women who feel so threatened by the changes that have already happened in our society that they're afraid, and they impede our efforts rather than assist. Enlightened and committed men like Alan Alda are essential, and it is through their help that we'll succeed.

In Alan's mind,

The real reason the Equal Rights Amendment is running into problems is not that there are legal questions but that the shaky foundations on which a lot of interpersonal relationships are based are being questioned. It's supposed to *look* like big strong men are protecting dependent, delicate women. But the master suffers as much as the slave, although not always in a way that's visible.
There are some species of ants that are so highly developed, they cannot feed themselves. They rely on soldier ants they steal from neighboring colonies to feed them. That level of dependency is the same that men have with women. I think the people who are against the ERA are raising the consciousness of everybody because they're saying, "Do you mean to say that this is going to lead to a situation where we're going to have to relate to one another as *people?* How dare you!

For Alan Alda it all comes together; for him the key relationship is marriage.

It's through the marriage relationship, or the life-partner relationship, that you can understand all behavior [he says]. It's

such hard work and it requires you to be so vulnerable. If you
don't do it well, you suffer, you hurt. And it keeps hurting.
But if you can work on it, then you can get along with a lot
of different kinds of people.

Alan Alda works on it. To him it's worth it; he's in it
for the things that last.

REFLECTIONS ON THE CHANGED WORLD [4]

The last ten years have seen so many changes in the
world that we who have lived through them all may well
feel—and fear—that we are getting numb. "Future shock"
has replaced "The Sense of the Past," which Henry James
celebrated and which does indeed have great value when
it nurtures an awareness of life as a continuing process, an
awareness that assumes a relationship of some kind, not
necessarily a simple linear one, between prior and present
events. . . .

Some changes are bigger than others. You can, if you
want, call a revolution a fad—in fact, that's a normal human reaction to revolution. But calling it a fad won't make
it go away. Among the multifarious novelties of the last
decade can be found a few which are major and permanent.

One grand change, perhaps the grandest, is our growing
awareness that a presence which had been knocking for a
century or more on the door of consciousness has entered
the world and shows no sign of leaving. God knows it's
been given a cool enough welcome, the awkward creature,
and no wonder. Balky and shy at times, it's unnervingly
indiscreet at others and will disturb the most sophisticated
by its habit of talking too much or laughing at unexpected
moments. Worse still, no one can be sure when it may
burst into outrageous threats or dissolve in tears of rage for
no clear reason. Older inhabitants, who have resigned them-

⁴ Excerpt from *Between Myth and Morning*, by Elizabeth Janeway, author
and lecturer. Morrow. '74. p 1-13. Reprinted by permission of William Morrow
& Company, Inc. Copyright © 1972, 1973, 1974 by Elizabeth Janeway.

selves philosophically to man's fate and curbed their own
desires, often find it greedy, and even those who declare
they are open-minded object to the way it mutters to itself
instead of speaking up in forthright, understandable terms.
Its demands have been declared by experts to be contradictory and overweening, quite out of the question for any
well-ordered system to live with. And yet—

It is still here. Neither mockery nor attack has banished
it, and paying lip service to its wishes, the next political
step, seems merely to encourage it to formulate more. Like
a fragment of nightmare, like a character from Beckett or
Ionesco, the creature has not only moved in, it keeps growing. It hardly has a name, for it runs uncontrollably over
the bounds of any neat definition. Women's Lib? Worn
out at the beginning by its pejorative intent. This creature
doesn't *care* if it's laughed at and opposition is only what
it expects. Feminism? Yes, but humanism too. The Wom-
en's Movement? Better, but still too structured. "Movement" implies direction, and this being has no more artic-
ulated, coherent view of its goals than a baby does. Its
goals and its acts are the same—growth, realization, discovery. Yet here it is, named or not. It is consciousness, it is
presence, it is woman wakened from a millennial slum-
ber. . . .

To say that this presence is new is an understatement.
When, a hundred-odd years ago, the pioneers of the Feminist Movement began to declare that women actually had
rights of their own, when they attacked and painfully
breached the walls surrounding "Woman's Place," they
were inaugurating an action which, as far as can be told,
had never before been undertaken in human history. Out
of the relics of thirty thousand years, there is no image of
woman that we can point to and say: This was made by
women alone, apart from the eyes or the direction of men.
Take the earliest images of all, the little "Venuses" of the
Old Stone Age which have been found across Europe and
Asia from the Atlantic littoral to Siberia. To name them

Venuses is to imply that they are goddesses; and so they have been called by many an archaeologist. But look at them with a human eye: they are not goddesses, they are fetishes, lucky pieces for a desperate man, hunter or hunted, starving or wounded, to thumb in time of need; a memory of Mum and Mum's protection and thus not a portrait of woman, but of man's need for her. They have neither faces nor feet, so they are neither present as individuals nor, denied autonomous motion, can they depart by themselves. Unlike the dancing shamans engraved or painted on the cave walls, they need no masks or disguises for they are masked in their own symbolism, fertility, as impenetrable to the mind and as much a part of natural existence as a breeding sow.

Even when the Goddess appears, her image is that of the woman seen by man from outside. She is the Great Mother, feared and adored, both mediator with and representative of necessity. This is not a picture drawn by woman. No girl child would form such an identity for herself, for there is nothing of her inner personal experience in it. . . . The Mother Goddess is an image shaped by emotions projected onto women, reflecting the desires and needs of others. In that pattern of making, a woman cannot be allowed to feel or express her own emotions, nor to originate any act, for her purpose is not to create her own life, but to validate the experience of others. *Her* experience isn't and can't be part of the reckoning, for it would confuse it hopelessly. It simply doesn't count and so she is absent from history.

This anonymity is part of her being, in Simone de Beauvoir's word, "other," for if she were not, if she could be seen as similar to men, she would have to be counted in. It is this quality of "otherness" which has engendered the familiar description of woman as enigma. It is, so to speak, a fallback line to be taken up when complete ignoring of her reality becomes impossible. Freud was demonstrating the value of this position in our own historical period when, years after the Feminist Movement had mounted its campaign for women's rights, he asked, "What does a woman want?" Over and over, before then and since, the question has been answered and the answer still goes unheard and unregarded. For to accept it—"A woman wants to be counted as human"—would entail accepting the full validity and equal significance of woman's wanting, woman's needs, woman's human presence; and thereby losing the blank mirror of otherness in which man searches for his face.

So it has been. Now this is ending. Over the last century or two, an instant of human time, women have begun to examine their own experience and to speak of what they find there. First the writers took up their pens. That was reasonably easy to do in niches and crannies of time as the age became literate, and it didn't require much in the way of equipment. A bottle of ink, a bundle of paper and a quill pen were not hard to come by and, as the middle class throve and increased, even women began to have a bit of leisure and privacy; enough to scribble in. Then, too, Romanticism conceived the idea that the individual personality was valuable in itself and though men might fail to assign such value to the female individual, women read the books too and were infected by the idea. Perhaps they had something to say!

Saying it in books had another attraction too. A woman could communicate her experience while invisible from her audience. Instead of being present in all her distracting femininity and disturbing otherness, she disappeared behind the printed page. In addition, the vogue of the novel stood women writers in good stead. No nineteenth century man could want to be preached at by a woman in a book of sermons, but he would hardly draw the line at being amused by one; entertaining the male had long been an acceptable part of the female role, as Scheherazade knew well. . . .

The painters were next. Indeed, women painters had

appeared as often as women poets, for their work too could
be sold or admired without their embarrassing presence.
Usually, however, they were apprenticed individually to
their trade by painter-fathers who lacked promising sons,
and they left no tradition and no protégées. Once more it
was the Romantically inspired nineteenth century which
found their work sentimentally pleasant and thus gave
them a general public. The cult of the home and the family made a place for the recording of women's experience.
But how many paintings, even by fine women artists, concentrate on the saleable, limited, *proper* female experience: Mary Cassatt's tea tables, Berthe Morisot's mothers
and children. Before Käthe Kollwitz, what woman painted
pain, horror or despair? Only the mad. Now, finally, the
dramatists and choreographers and filmmakers and com-
posers, artists who cannot work alone and have been dependent on the willingness of others (men) to mount their
work, are beginning to be seen and heard. At last, at last,
our self-portraits are being created across the breadth of
art. . . .

The appearance of women artists is a strong vital sign
of the new presence in the world.

Not that women have never created art before; only that
it has always been anonymous. Women's art in the past
was folk art: beautiful, moving and communicating a great
deal about their lives, but always adapted to functions and
purposes set by society. Only in the last few seconds of historical time, last century, this century, have women been
allowed to be individual artists speaking with their own
voices, soloists apart from the choir.

Consequently the experience of women has not only
been structured by men, it has been given its significance
by men. Men have said, "This is true and that is false;
this is right and that is wrong"; and, most important of
all, they have said, "This is important and that is secondary." They have told us even what it is that has happened
to us, named the events of our lives. Not all men have

had a hand in this, naturally, for such ordering of reality is effected by the powerful, and not all men have a grasp on power. But there is no period we know of in which the powerful have not been men, even when they have made and held to a bargain with the weak. So women have learned to judge their lives and to identify their emotions according to an external determination. It will be a long time yet before we understand all that means, for first we have a great deal to unlearn. We aren't even sure who we are. Barely awake, still rubbing our eyes, we are stunned by the idea that we might say Yes and No because of our own wants and needs, not someone else's. When have we dared to do that without first asking ourselves, "What will they think of me? Isn't it wrong and unwomanly for me to imagine that what I want can be as important as what he wants? Won't I pay for such selfishness, such shameful exposure of my desires, such illicit wants, by bringing down on my head the disapproval of the powerful? And the envy and distrust of other women, who will surely resent any rebel who dares to value herself as the equal of the men they've attached themselves to and are dependent on?" So at the very outset we are tangling with the social imperatives inherent in our society, and with the mythology which justifies them and goes on to direct the fashion in which we live and behave and conceive ourselves.

Thus the awakening and the start on reinterpreting experience, the daring to judge oneself worthy of making judgments and also the coming together with other women as friends and sharers of life instead of as rivals for approval by men—all this is going on at once. That is confusing, but it is a fruitful confusion, in which one aspect of life runs into another. As an example, take this business of sharing, or "bonding," to use Lionel Tiger's phrase. When Tiger declared that men came together into groups and women did not he was, broadly speaking, an accurate reporter of circumstances, though in some societies women find joint action less difficult than in others. Thus, the anthropologist Victor Turner reports of a Zambian people he has studied for many years: "Most Ndembu, both men and women, were members of at least one cult association, and it was hard to find an elderly person who was not an 'expert' in the secret knowledge of more than one cult." Among the Ndembu, too, ceremonies exist in which the whole group of women oppose the men, with each sex singing ribald and jeering songs about the other, though the ambience is one of high good humor: "The whole atmosphere is buoyant and aggressively jovial, as men and women strive to shout one another down."

If women have not joined together for jovial shouting matches more often, the reason does not lie in sex-related genetic coding, for if it did, such variant examples as the Ndembu could hardly exist. Rather it is long-term patterns of living which have isolated women from each other by making them subordinate to men, and thus individually dependent on men. . . .

Isolation, nonetheless, has been a constant feature of past societies, for women's access to power has always been more or less vicarious, and has had to take a personal route. A woman acts through, or on, a man and her success is ultimately based on her ability to please and persuade. This is not a quality to be belittled, nor is a pleasant and persuasive character to be reprobated, though it need not, surely, be recommended only to women. Pleasant men are pleasant company too. The difficulty comes when the power to please and persuade becomes the *only* road to action, when power must be attained through the show of weakness. If women are called deceptive and not straightforward, it is because of this bind which tells us that if we are going to act at all, we must manipulate the man we are supposed to be pleasing. We know that we have, in the past, pleased most easily when we have accepted, introjected and acted out, *as if spontaneously,* the role in which society cast us. Spontaneity, sincerity, then, become instruments for deception. Virtue itself is smudged by being "useful." And always when the good woman is defined as pleasing others, her own pleasure must come from them, so that everything is reflected and nothing direct.

This is obviously the road to lonely rivalry with other women, not to bonding in sisterhood. Bonding involves a promise to act together and to be responsible with others in action. In turn, this demands that one trust oneself to be that responsible creature. Can we trust ourselves? The way in which women have been disvalued by society has persuaded us to disvalue ourselves. But suddenly, in these last awakening years, the tables have turned. By trusting each other, we find we can trust ourselves. As we value other women more highly we can gain self-confidence. Then bonds begin to form and to strengthen us, for confidence and self-confidence interact powerfully, working together toward greater interior solidity and also toward a kind of comfortable at-homeness in the world. One of the unexpected bonuses of liberation for women is an increased capacity to enjoy oneself in one's own way, to be the pleased person instead of the one who is expected to do the pleasing....

I believe that the societal restraints imposed on women by the stereotypes of our culture have cost us an enormous amount of psychic energy. How much talent and capacity must have been wasted in holding our impulses down, in molding our behavior to match the ideal our consciences held up as appropriate to The Good Woman! How often and how intensely we have quarreled with ourselves when we began to feel the urge to act in some insidious, unwomanly way, just because it would be pleasing to us, instead of being good for others! And such repressions, be it noted, have contributed to the compulsion among women to be private and secret, for these transgressions have seemed like sins, inadmissible even to our dear friends; or, if admitted, forming a private and almost illicit bond: we two evildoers and upholders of subversion. Once again, large bonding for action, easy friendship between free people, is prevented. Only as the stereotypes have faded and the barriers to enjoyment have gone down have the barriers to friendships fallen too. Almost automatically the bonding that never happened has begun to form. Nor are such friendships confined to friendships with women, by the way, for being easy and open with others can mean openness to affectionate friendship with men too.

What has freed women today is not, of course, the act of any God or any Goddess either. We have been given a chance at liberation by the workings of historical forces; specifically, by the disruption and overthrow of old patterns of life through the intervention of profound and long-term economic, technological and scientific processes. All revolutions come about through the cracking open of social patterns and systems so that, previously inhibited human capacities can come into play. That's as true of a cultural revolution (the Renaissance) as it is of the overthrow of empires (the barbarian invasions which finally brought a weakened Rome to its end). Nor can culture and politics and economics and technology be separated: all work together. The women's revolution, or movement or liberation—it will find its name one day!—is not unique, nor is it a thing in itself, set apart in our time from the other effects of change.

Certainly it was not set in motion originally by women. It is a response to a whole intermeshed collection of changing pressures and processes, to other revolutionary social changes, to the decreasing economic function of the family, to schooling outside the home and to the public images that flood into the home via radio and television, to the new sort of homes people live in, to the Pill and what it means for the planning of childbirth, to medical advances that have ended the commonplace death of children in their first years of life (and so helped both to boom the population and to produce a reaction to the threat of uncontrolled population growth), to migration and mobility within a society both up and down and geographically, cross-country, to machines that have made physical strength unimportant, to higher education for more than the few—there is really no place to end the list. The modern world has made the Women's Movement, made it possible and now inevitable. What women are doing now is making the downfall or decline of the Movement clearly impossible. That awkward new presence in the world is here to stay. . . .

What is happening to women involves a sudden enlargement of our world: the sky above us lifts, light pours in. Certainly that illumination reveals fear, anger and frustration, doubt and uncertainty. Confusion reigns. If we have an idea where we want to go (and we do) we are not at all sure how to get there. No maps exist for this enlarged world, we must make them as we explore, and we are not even sure we know how. We must muster our strengths, both old and new. We shall need patience and courage and endurance; stamina is the best word, I think. These are the familiar virtues of woman's place. But in addition we must learn some new ones, what I called (in *Man's World, Woman's Place*) "the prince's virtues of daring, honor and panache."

Add some unlearning of old assets. We need to be able to call on egotistic, stubborn persistence in the face of disagreement, to be right rather than pleasing. All this means a breaking away from the old role, and it isn't easy. Much of the internal distress recorded in recent books by women who are wakening to history and the world of events, and dwelt on obsessively by disconcerted men, is occasioned by the pull of these new needs against the tug of the old image assigned so long ago, in which we have striven so hard to shape ourselves, the image of the Good Woman, loving and giving and loved for her giving. Although she is a construct of others, although she demands submission and withdrawal and vicarious living, although we know her demands have become crippling, we have lived with her and tried to live *as* her for a long time. Giving her up is frightening, seems to leave the world barren. *Can* we replace her image? Can we trust this awkward, amorphous, unnamed creature who has invaded our consciousness and our lives to shape herself into a new ideal?

I believe we can, and one reason I do is that central to the experience of women coming together as friends and allies is *recognition*. We have been alone for a long time. . . . Recognition: one finds oneself in others. One feels a coming together, one talks with the confidence of being understood. But mark well that what we are finding is not simply common femininity. It is something much wider, infinitely extensive under that lifted sky above our heads. It is common *humanity*. It is the right to say, "I belong here. I am part of the whole, I understand." Distrust runs off the surface of the world like receding floodwater. Euphoric, intoxicating, transient—yes, even the uplifted heart knows that its joy must be reckoned as all those things, but neither should the experience be ignored or disvalued. Like the Ndembu women Victor Turner witnessed, we have found a way of singing together.

Considering that emotion and others like it experienced by other groups, Turner has adapted Martin Buber's *community* to the form *communitas*. "At certain life crises," he writes, "such as adolescence, the attainment of elderhood, and death, varying in significance from culture to culture, the passage from one structural status to another may be accomplished by a strong sentiment of 'humankindness,' a sense of the generic social bond between all members of society." In the life crisis of contemporary women, this bond supports us as we move to adult responsibility. If the euphoria dims, as it will, the mood has still left its mark in memory and something of the exhilaration remains within our grasp. To find oneself suddenly free to use one's full strength is intoxicating. The first burst of delight will pass, but the joy of using that strength, of facing the world and its facts and problems and dangers and difficulties in the knowledge that one can tackle it with a whole heart and undivided mind and comradeship with others, that remains. I wish that sense of joy in one's own useful energy and in one's connection with others to everyone in this world.

BIBLIOGRAPHY

An asterisk (*) preceding a reference indicates that the article or a part of it has been reprinted in this book.

BOOKS

Ardrey, Robert. African genesis. Atheneum. '61.

Bardwick, Judith and others. Feminine personality and conflict. Brooks/Cole. '73.

Beauvoir, Simone de. The second sex; tr & ed by H. M. Parshley. Knopf. '52.

Bednarik, Karl. The male in crisis. Knopf. '70.

Bengis, Ingrid. Combat in the erogenous zone. Knopf. '72.

Bernard, J. S. The future of marriage. World. '72.

*Bird, Caroline. Born female: the high cost of keeping women down. McKay. '68.

Chafetz, J. S. Masculine/feminine or human? Peacock. '74.

Chesler, Phyllis. Women and madness. Doubleday. '72.

Davis, E. G. The first sex. Putnam. '71.

Decter, Midge. The new chastity and other arguments against women's liberation. Coward, McCann & Geoghegan. '72.

Donelson, Elaine and Gullahorn, J. E. Women: a psychological perspective. Wiley. '77.

Erikson, E. H. Childhood and society. 2d ed rev and enl Norton. '64.

Fox, Robin. Kinship and marriage. Penguin. '67.

Friedan, Betty. The feminine mystique. Norton. '63.

*Friedan, Betty. It changed my life: writings on the women's movement. Random House. '76.

Gilder, G. F. Sexual suicide. Quadrangle. '73.

Goldberg, Steven. The inevitability of patriarchy. Morrow. '73.

Greer, Germaine. The female eunuch. McGraw-Hill. '71.

Guttentag, Marcia and Bray, Helen. Undoing sex stereotypes: research & resources for education. McGraw-Hill. '76.

*Harrison, B. G. Unlearning the lie: sexism in school. Liveright. '73.

Heilbrun, C .G. Toward a recognition of androgyny. Knopf. '73.

Hennig, Margaret and Jardim, Anne. The managerial woman. Doubleday. '77.
    Review article entitled: For ambitious women, a survival guide to the land of bosses. Nan Robertson. New York Times. p 50. Je. 28, '77.

Horney, Karen. Feminine psychology. Norton. '67.

Howe, L. K. comp. The future of the family. Simon & Schuster. '72.

*Janeway, Elizabeth. Between myth and morning. Morrow. '74.

Janeway, Elizabeth. Man's world, woman's place: a study in social mythology. Morrow. '71.

Klagsbrun, Francine, ed. The first Ms. reader. Warner Books. '73.

*Korda, Michael. Male chauvinism! how it works. Random House. '73.

Lewis, C. S. The abolition of man. Macmillan. '47.

*Lorand, R. L. Letter to Minnesota Committee for Positive Education. The author. 40 Central Park South. New York, NY 10019. '75.

Maccoby, E. E. and Jacklin, Carol. The psychology of sex differences. Stanford University Press. '74.

*McGraw-Hill Book Company. Guidelines for equal treatment of the sexes in McGraw-Hill Book Company publications. ['74]

Mailer, Norman. The prisoner of sex. Little, Brown. '71.

May, Rollo. Power and innocence. Norton. '72.

Mead, Margaret. Male and female: a study of the sexes in a changing world. Dell. '68.

Mead, Margaret. Sex and temperament in three primitive societies. Dell. '68.

Mednick, M. S. and others, eds. Women and achievement: social and motivational analyses. Halsted Press. '75.

Mill, J. S. and Taylor, Harriet. Essays on sex equality; ed by A. S. Rossi. rev ed University of Chicago Press. '70.

*Miller, Casey and Swift, Kate. Words and women. (Anchor Books) Doubleday. '76.

Millett, Kate. Sexual politics. Doubleday. '70.

Montagu, Ashley. The natural superiority of women. new rev ed Collier. '74.

Morgan, Elaine. The descent of woman. Stein & Day. '72.

Morgan, Marabel. The total woman. Revell. '73.

Morris, Desmond. The naked ape. Dell. '69.

*New York City Commission on Human Rights. Women's role in contemporary society; report, Sept. 21-25, 1970. Avon Books. '72.

   Reprinted in this book: Women's rights: a cultural dilemma. Margaret Mead. p 172-83.

O'Neill, Nena and O'Neill, George. Open marriage. Avon. '73.

*Packard, Vance. The sexual wilderness. McKay. '68.

Peck, Ellen. The baby trap. Bernard Geis Associates. '71.

Pleck, J. H. and Sawyer, Jack, eds. Men and masculinity. Prentice-Hall. '74.

Reich, Wilhelm. The sexual revolution; new tr by Therese Pol. Simon & Schuster. '74.

Richardson, H. W. Nun, witch, playmate; the Americanization of sex. Harper & Row. '71.

Rosaldo, M. Z. and Lamphore, Louise, eds. Women, culture, and society. Stanford University Press. '74.

*Schlafly, Phyllis. The power of the positive woman. Arlington House. '77.

Sexton, P. C. The feminized male: classrooms, white collars and the decline of manliness. Random House. '69.

Stacey, Judith and others, eds. And Jill came tumbling after: sexism in American education. Dell. '74.

*Stapleton, Jean and Bright, Richard. Equal marriage. Abingdon. '76.

Stassinopoulos, Arianna. The female woman. Random House. '74.

Tiger, Lionel. Men in groups. Vintage Books. '70.

Toffler, Alvin. Future shock. Random House, '70.

United States. Department of Health, Education, and Welfare. Office for Civil Rights. Final Title 9 regulation implementing education amendments of 1972, prohibiting sex discrimination in education, effective date, July 21, 1975. The Office. '75.

Vilar, Esther. The manipulated man. Farrar, Straus. '72.

PERIODICALS

American Journal of Sociology. 77:1128-46. My. '72. Sex-role socialization in picture books for pre-school children. L. J. Weitzman and others.

Atlantic. 227:39-50. My. '71. The obsolescent mother. Edward Grossman.

*Christian Century. 92:260-2+. Mr. 12, '75. Television: Marcus Welby or Archie Bunker—will the real chauvinist pig please stand up? Carol Christ.

*Editorials on File. 6:384-7. Ap. 1-15, '75. Supreme Court ends discrimination between Social Security benefits.
   Editorials reprinted in this volume: Post-Tribune [March 8, 1975. Gary, Ind.]. p 386; Arizona Republic [March 26, 1975. Phoenix]. p 387.

*Editorials on File. 6:641-7. Je. 1-15, '75. Sex bias in schools barred by new Administration rules.
   Editorials reprinted in this volume: Providence (R.I.) Journal (June 8, 1975]. p 643; Salt Lake Tribune [June 5, 1975]. p 644.

*Editorials on File. 6:1370-4. N. 1-15, '75. N.Y., N.J. voters defeat state ERA.
   Editorials reprinted in this volume: Pittsburgh Post-Gazette [November 8, 1975]. p 1372; Los Angeles Times [November 12, 1975] p 1372.

234

The Reference Shelf

English Journal 64:16-18. N. '75. Androgeny [sic] test—multiple choice. Norma Willson.

Esquire. 75:82-5+. Ja. '71. The feminine mistake. Helen Lawrenson.

Esquire. 76:87-9+. O. '71. She. Leonard Levitt.

Esquire. 78:95-8+. O. '72. What is the new impotence, and who's got it? Philip Nobile.

Esquire. 80:71-5+. Jl. '73. Foremothers. Sara Davidson.

Harper's Bazaar. 108:52+. Jl. '75. What makes a good father? Sol Gordon.

Harper's Magazine. 243:35-9. Jl.; 7-8. S. '71. The surprising seventies. P. F. Drucker.

Harper's Magazine. 251:93. Jl. '75. Prisoner of gender. Sam Julty.

*Horizon. 19:40-5. My. '77. Why men and women think differently. Kenneth Lamott.

Journal of Educational Psychology. 66 no 2:157-66. '74. Sex bias in the evaluation of professional achievements. H. N. Mischel.

Journal of Personality. 41:9-13. '73. The relationship between role orientation and achievement motivation in college women. T. G. Alper.

Journal of Personality and Social Psychology. 29.80-5. '74. Explanations of successful performance on sex-linked tasks: what is skill for the male is luck for the female. Kay Deaux and Tim Emsweiler.

Journal of Social Issues. 28 no 2:129-55. '72. Early childhood experiences and women's achievement motives. L. W. Hoffman.

Journal of Social Issues. 28 no 2:157-75. '72. Toward an understanding of achievement-related conflicts in women. M. S. Horner.

Long Island Press. p 15. Mr. 16, '77. Abuses of office dictators.

Ms. 1:78-81+. Jl. '72. Competing with women. Letty Cottin Pogrebin.

Ms. 1:82-3+. D. '72. Money is the root of all freedom? Caroline Bird.

Ms. 4:41-2. My. '76. Part-time work: when less is more. C. S. Greenwald.

*National Review. 27:887. Ag. 15, '75. Unisex and the public schools. Russell Kirk.

National Review. 27:1096. O. 10, '75. Women with guns [editorial].

National Review. 27:1118. O. 10, '75. On toying with desecration. M. B. Martin.

New Times. p 40+. Ja. '77. Androgeny [sic]. Andrew Kopkind.

*New York Times. p 48. Ap. 10, '74. A matter of identity: women who keep their maiden names. Judy Klemesrud.

*New York Times. p 1. S. 12, '76. Women entering job market at an "extraordinary" pace. Robert Lindsey.

New York Times. p 11. Ap. 8, '77. Panel of historians calls for a shift in research to emphasize central role of women in history. Wayne King.

New York Times Magazine. p 26-7+. Mr. 19, '72. Is Women's lib a passing fad? Joseph Adelson.

New York Times Magazine. p 10-11+. S. 5, '76. Kill, hate—mutilate! [women at the Air force academy]. Grace Lichtenstein.

Oregon ASCD Curriculum Bulletin. 31:6-20. Ap. '77. A survey of recent studies in sex roles. Millicent Rutherford.

Psychiatric News. 10:11. Je. 18, '75. Women and men said to differ in their response to stress. Marianne Frankenhaeuser.

*Psychiatry. 4:1-8. '41. The role of women in this culture. Clara Thompson.
    Slightly revised version reprinted in Women and analysis, ed. by Jean Strouse. Viking. '75. p 265-77.

Psychological Bulletin. 80 no 5:345-66. '73. Socialization of achievement orientation in females. A. H. Stein and M. M. Bailey.

Psychological Bulletin. 80 no 5:389-407. '73. Masculinity-Femininity: an exception to a famous dictum? Anne Constantinople.

Psychology Today. 3:36-8+. N. '69. Fail: bright women. M. S. Horner.

Psychology Today. 8:85+. Ja. '75. Stereotyping—it starts early and dies hard. Jack Horn.

Psychology Today. 9:58+. D. '75. It's tough to nip sexism in the bud; study by Marcia Guttentag. Carol Tavris.

*Reader's Digest. 107:138-41. S. '75. Why men won't seek help. J. L. Collier.

Redbook. 143:51-2. My. '74. What worries me most about Women's lib. Judith Viorst.

Redbook. 145:38+. Je. '75. Is it true what they say about Southern women? Florence King.

Redbook. 146:58+. Ja. '76. What makes a man feel loved? Avery Corman.

*Redbook. 147:88+. Jl. '76. Alan Alda: America's sweetheart. Susan Edmiston.

Redbook. 147:45+. S. '76. How men feel about the way they look. Judith Viorst.

Saturday Review. 2:12-14+. Je. 14, '75. International Women's Year special section.
    Sex, society, and the female dilemma—a dialogue between Simone de Beauvoir and Betty Friedan. p 14+; Men's words, women's roles, by Dan Lacy. p 25+; Needed: full partnership for women, by Margaret Mead. p 26-7.

Saturday Review. 4:6-13+. Je. 25, '77. Women against women: special report.

Saturday Review of the Society. 1:60-2+. My. '73. Sex as athletics in the singles complex. Cynthia Proulx.

*Science Digest. 77:10-15. Ja. '75. Superbowl time in the battle of the sexes. Gurney Williams III.

*Science Digest. 80:8-9. Ag. '76. Women are their own worst friends.

Science News. 107:238. Ap. 12, '75. Stress on the sexes: how they differ.

*Science News. 108:173-4. S. 13, '75. Sexism is depressing; study by Marcia Guttentag. R. J. Trotter.

Science News. 108:246. O. 18, '75. Male students still better in science.

Scientific American. 226:34-9. Ja. '72. How ideology shapes women's lives. Jean Lipman-Blumen.

Social Policy. 3:11-19. S.-O. '72. Implications for women. C. S. Bell.

Sports Illustrated. 38:88-92+. My. 28, '73. Sport is unfair to women. Bil Gilbert and Nancy Williamson.

Sports Illustrated. 38:44-8+. Je. 4, '73. Are you being two-faced? Bil Gilbert and Nancy Williamson.

Sports Illustrated. 38:60-2+. Je. 11, '73. Programmed to be losers. Bil Gilbert and Nancy Williamson.

Today's Health. 53:38-41+. My. '75. Motherhood is not my game. Claire Safran.

Today's Health. 53:14-17. O. '75. What we're finding out about sexual stereotypes. Claire Safran.

UNESCO Courier. 28:58-61. Ag. '75. Masculine, feminine or neutral? A. I. Belkin.

*U.S. News & World Report. 79:54. O. 20, '75. Girls lag on tests: unequal education?

*U.S. News & World Report. 81:8. S. 27, '76. Women in the clergy: another barrier falls.

*U.S. News & World Report. 81:79-82. S. 27, '76. How to make the most of today's opportunities: interview. B. S. Greiff.

Village Voice. p 13. Jl. 26, '76. The price of paying your own way. Vivian Gornick.